Islam and Social Policy

Islam and Social Policy

Edited by
Stephen P. Heyneman

Vanderbilt University Press

Nashville

This book is printed on acid-free paper.

Manufactured in the United States of America

Library of Congress Cataloging-in-Publication Data

Islam and social policy / edited by Stephen P. Heyneman.

1st ed.

p. cm.

Includes bibliographical references and index.

ISBN 0-8265-1446-4 (cloth : alk. paper)

ISBN 0-8265-1447-2 (pbk. : alk. paper)

    1. Sociology, Islamic. 2. Islam-Social aspects. 3. Islam-

Charities. 4. Islam and social problems.

I. Heyneman, Stephen P. II. Title.

BP173.25I738 2004

297.2'7-dc22

                            2003017648

Contents

Introduction   1
Stephen P. Heyneman

1   **The Islamic Institution of Waqf:
A Historical Overview**   13
Ahmad Dallal

2   **Islamic Law and the Position of Women**   44
Donna Lee Bowen

3   **Islamic Law and Family Planning**   118
Donna Lee Bowen

4   **Islamic Law and Zakat:
Waqf Resources in Pakistan**   156
Gail Richardson

5   **Islam and Health Policy:
A Study of the Islamic Republic of Iran**   181
Carol Underwood

Glossary of Arabic Terms   207

Contributors   213

Index   215

Introduction

Stephen P. Heyneman

These essays constitute a conscious effort to explain how Islam sees itself in terms of social policy. By social policy, we mean how Islam treats women, how it encourages charity, education, and general social welfare. By "Islam," in this context, we mean many things. We mean the historical precedents of Islamic religious law and how it is organized currently. We include the many regional cultures in which Islam is situated and which influence its social policy. And we include too, examples of state policies, past and present, that help determine how Islamic law is treated. We mean all these things.

The point of this volume is to give the reader *un tour d'horizon*, an overview of some of the most delicate issues that societies need to face: how to treat the poor, promote charity, and establish fair relations among communities and within families. The essays attempt to provide an explanation for some of the more poignant sources of misunderstanding between Islamic and Western cultures: Is it true that females bear the brunt of discrimination? Why are there so many different charitable and educational foundations, and why do some become legally controversial, bypassing their stated charitable objectives? The volume points out both the similarities between Islamic and Western cultures in terms of social aspirations and basic religious principles and the significant differences in their cultural assumptions.

1

We commissioned these essays originally for use by staff of development assistance agencies with responsibilities in Muslim countries, including the World Bank, the International Monetary Fund (IMF), and other organizations under the auspices of the United Nations—UNESCO, UNICEF, WHO, ILO, and so forth. We hope that they will benefit staff of bilateral (country-to-country) organizations and international nongovernmental organizations that seek to offer assistance in terms of social welfare, human rights, education, and gender equality.

Each author utilizes a wide range of skills and scholarly experience. Donna Lee Bowen employs her deep understanding of Morocco and her training in both political science and anthropology, Ahmad Dallal his knowledge of Islamic history, Carol Underwood her understanding of public health and her long field experience in Iran, and Gail Richardson her skills at exploring the complex operational mechanisms of public social welfare bureaucracies.

Synopsis

From the essay, "Waqf: An Historical Overview," one might derive several lessons. In that all social classes, races, and ethnic groups are treated equally, Islam is a religion of absolute equality. But, as importantly, because inheritance from one generation to the next is carefully prescribed, one can say that Islam also represents a system of wealth redistribution.

Essential to all religions, charity is also a central organizing principle in Islam. What Ahmad Dallal teaches us is how charity is organized. The closest analogy to the system of Islamic *awqaf* (plural of *waqf*) might be the Western concept of a foundation, in which an endowment is set aside in perpetuity for certain specified purposes.

The concept of awqaf was created by Abraham in 1860 B.C.E. and was common well before Islam was founded. What makes the system of awqaf so interesting is that it was often utilized to circumvent the restrictions on intergenerational inheritance. Ahmad Dallal describes this nefarious (but understandable) tradition and uses this part of the story to introduce the reader to the system of Islamic courts in which such problems were adjudicated. His essay includes references to court findings concerning the conditions for becoming a legitimate founder of a waqf, the role of an administrator, and the legitimate uses for waqf revenue—municipal public works, religious education, food for the poor, and assistance to the infirm, the aged, and the mentally handicapped. He traces the legal history over a thousand years and points out how important awqaf traditions have been for women to pass on their wealth to charitable causes, how important the system has been simply in terms of size. In the eighteenth century, over half the population of several Ottoman cities were fed by awqaf revenues, over 20 percent of Egypt's arable land was set aside for awqaf endowments and significant projects in support of cathedral mosques, markets, and other forms of urban revitalization.

The essay also traces how the tradition of awqaf was treated first by European colonial authorities, then by Islamic colonial authorities (such as the Ottomans), and, lastly, by the post-WWII nation-states. In each instance, having a considerable level of resources independently allocated became a source of tension and conflict, and in each instance, there were attempts to control, guide, and outright expropriate.

Though problems across the ages and geographical regions were not identical, many were common: the use of awqaf to avoid state taxes, circumvent laws on inheritance, and, on occasion, support heretical ideologies.

In her essay, "Islamic Law and the Treatment of Women," Donna Lee Bowen takes up the discussion of Islamic courts where the previous essay left off. As a preamble, she introduces the reader to the sources of Islamic legal opinion (revelations, words and actions [Sunna] and the compilation of texts [hadith]; the five levels of Islamic action (obligatory, recommended, permissible, reprehensible, and prohibited), and the four schools of Sunni Islamic law (Maliki, Hanafi, Shafi'i, and Hanbali) and the Shi'a schools, here considered as one.[1]

She explains how pre-Islamic cultural traditions have influenced each of these five traditions and how legal opinion differs among them, in part because of the differing local cultural heritages. Although there is strong commonality across the five Islamic legal traditions, she explains that there are important differences of interpretation. Since the five legal traditions are associated with different regions, Islamic legal opinion therefore differs considerably in Morocco, Iran, Indonesia, and Saudi Arabia. For the inexperienced but interested outside observer, Bowen provides a geographical road map to the variations in Islamic social policy, even before raising the main topic under her scrutiny, the position and treatment of women.

Once her discussion of gender is launched, the reader will better understand many issues of Islamic family law: the duties of the husband, the regulation of bride-price,[2] and the principles of marriage, divorce, child custody, and inheritance. She also summarizes popular opinion among modern Muslims about family law and divides them into six categories: traditionalists, feminists, secularists, activists, reformers, and those who follow customary practice.

While there are many lessons to be derived from her essay, there is one that deserves particularly close attention: why the position of women in Islam is not based on equality, but rather on equity. Bowen helps us to understand that—since the time of the reformation—the principle of equality in Western law has been based on the rights and obligations of each individual. Islamic law, however, takes the family unit as the principal unit of responsibility rather than the individual. The daughter inherits less than the son, but this is taken to be just because the son is obligated to financial responsibilities to support family elders, orphans, and widows. Though it is not equal, neither is it unjust.

What lesson can the reader draw? Some readers may begin

to question whether it is right for Western feminists to argue for equal rights for individuals at the expense of the rights of families, and whether abrogating the rights of families may threaten a nation's social cohesion. They might well ask where moral authority originates or whether there are alternative—and equally compelling—principles of justice than that of equal individual rights.

If there is a single issue on which Islamic feminists agree it is that the feminism—as defined by the West—may have ancillary implications, with crippling effects on the health of the family, the principal organizing unit for all civilized societies (Esposito 1982; Fernea 1998; Mahdavi 1985; Moghadam 1993; Mueller 1985). Bowen's point is that Western definitions of gender equality can be destructive to more important constructs, and that gender equity (based on judgment of fairness rather than the proof of identical distribution) can be more sensible as well as more just.

In her following essay, "Islamic Law and Family Planning," Bowen again provides the reader with a necessary foundation on the sources of evidence for Islamic law, the distribution of different legal schools, and how each interprets legal texts with respect to 'azl (contraception), including questions of infanticide, abortion, and other birth-control methods.

She points out several things worthy of note, particularly with respect to the modern governmental approaches to Islam described in the next two essays. She observers differences in the role of the imam (clergy) between the Sunni and the Shi'a communities. For the Sunni, the imam may lead a congregation in prayer, but this implies neither high education nor professional expertise. For the Shi'a, the imam is connected with the descendents of those who succeeded Muhammad and, hence, has a proscribed level of authority. This theme is a central focus in the later essay by Carol Underwood who describes Iran as the only instance in the Islamic world where there is a central religious system endowed with hierarchical moral authority.

Another point raised by Bowen indicates how Islamic law can

be politicized. Al-Azhar, the great theological center of learning in Cairo, was influential in the 1960s in persuading the public to plan families in a healthier manner by limiting births to a number that could be supported financially. But radical Islamic groups argued in the 1980s against birth control on grounds that it leads to a woman's immorality and represented a conspiracy on the part of the unpopular (and ungodly) national governments and development assistance agencies in their effort to subvert Islam by limiting the size of the Islamic population.[3] So popular has this radical (and paranoid) view become that support for this aspect of social policy depends largely on how it is phrased. "Contraception" is unpopular but "family planning" is popular. The difference hinges on the belief that one contributes to unbridled individuality and the other to a stronger family unit.

These "political" orientations are not limited to the public at large but are mirrored by differences within religious authorities themselves. The more sophisticated ('ulama) tend to resemble professors of history, religion, linguistics, and law. They tend to have more tolerant views of family planning. Religious leaders on a local level (imam) act as Qur'anic school and kindergarten instructors and vary considerably in the quality of their training and, hence, in the conservatism of their family planning opinions.

Bowen's two essays require the reader to give thought to several challenging theses. She argues that Islamic law provides a "flexibility and elegance" on sensitive questions—the value of marriage, the importance of contracts, the inviolability of life, and the balance of rights and responsibilities between the individual, the family, and the wider community.

She points out something else. While, for the most part, Christian tradition ignores or forbids sexuality, Islamic law recognizes and tries to manage it. The sexual side of man's nature and the necessity for a healthy family provide the intellectual foundation for polygamy. Thus the social order is supported by strengthening marriage rather than being undermined by allowing adultery. The point is not whether this line of reasoning is to be declared right or wrong. Bowen's points is that it has a compelling internal logic that we should understand and appreciate for its virtues.

One final issue: Donna Lee Bowen acknowledges that those who question Muslim women about their status can be perplexed by the variety of views they find. She believes that this is due to two factors. One is the tendency for traditional Muslim behaviors to be challenged by global forces that are out of their control (Muslim societies are not alone in this concern). But the second is more problematic still. She argues that, in spite of its traditional flexibility, there is an inability in Islamic legal mechanisms to redress the circumstances of victims and victimizer, that this contrasts starkly with Western law, and, since parallel Western legal systems are available in most Muslim countries, there is a crippling conflict between the two systems.

How is Islamic social policy treated by the modern state? Each essay includes a discussion of this, but the two final essays are dedicated to it. In her digging through the federal ministries in Pakistan, Gail Richardson discovered that there was a Ministry of Zakat (an Islamic tax on certain assets devoted to the poor) and Waqf. Her essay, "Zakat and Waqf Resources in Pakistan," describes what she found.[4]

She mentions that the *zakat* (2.5 percent tax on certain assets) was voluntary in Pakistan until 1980. Then it was made mandatory and divided into two categories depending on whether it was assessed at the point of source (bank accounts) or subject to self-assessment (gold, cash, stocks, and bonds). Funds are used for assistance to the needy, the handicapped, disabled, and widowed and to support health clinics dispensaries or *madrassas* (religious schools). There is a Central Zakat Council that specified that 40 percent of the funds be used for educational stipends and scholarships. Funds are collected by banks (both public and private), post offices, and other financial institutions "without charge."

Administrative expenses are paid by local governments and agencies though which many of the funds flow. She also describes the functions of the National Zakat Foundation, a semiautonomous branch of the Ministry of Finance that helps to construct buildings and purchase equipment, furniture, and vehicles. She also notes the tasks of the Awaqf Department, which has a Project Directorate dealing with planning, designing, and implementing charitable works.

This important and unexplored administrative labyrinth within the Pakistani government holds out the opportunity to effectively reach millions of the poor. But it also contains some profound dilemmas. One of them concerns the relationship between public and private institutions. To what extent do waqf-supported health clinics adhere to modern medical practice? Or more importantly, to what extent do the madrassas adhere to a national curriculum? As educational practice, instilling either political or religious extremism is reprehensible. But maintaining educational standards is not only a preoccupation of western nations; rather, it is a concern of all nations. Where there are examples of a rogue curriculum, regardless of whether it is financed by private charities or an extremist ethnic group, all people are affected (Heyneman 2000, 2002–2003). It can be a danger to its country of origin as well as to its neighbors.

But there is another side to the question of the public role, and that side is presented by Carol Underwood in her essay, "Islam and Health Policy: a Study of the Islamic Republic of Iran." As each author before her, she helps lay a historical foundation for the reader. First, she explains why the modernization efforts of the Shah and his Western supporters failed to have the expected health impact. Traditional ways, she says, were thought to inhibit development: "Tradition was juxtaposed to modernization." Modernization included technology, the distribution of pharmaceuticals, and urban hospitals. In spite of the fact that the majority of the population adhered to Islam, the health principles of Islam were not employed, but rather were treated as impediments to social change.

Carol Underwood tells a story of an extraordinary use of Islamic institutions to further public-health goals after the revolution. But she begins the story not with the revolution itself but with the intervention of Ali Shariati, the first to point out the potential of using Shi'ite ideology for revolutionary changes in public policy and the possibilities for using the network of mosques and universities to forge the necessary ingredients. This ability to combine religious Islamic education with Western empirical education, in her view, constituted a breakthrough.

In addition, she points to the unique effect of having an organization of mosques with a national hierarchy in which messages could be centralized from the Tehran health ministry through the religious headquarters in Qum to be simultaneously broadcast during Friday prayers. The messages were simple and compelling: immunization, potable water, breast-feeding, basic hygiene, literacy, the distribution of food coupons, goods for the needy, and the implementation of small health projects. The number of rural health clinics grew from eight hundred in 1976 to fifteen thousand in 2000; infant and child mortality dropped by 39 percent in the 1980s and by another 44 percent in the 1990s; and (as a result of the emphasis on family planning) the total fertility rate (number of live births per hundred women of childbearing age) declined from 6.4 in 1984 to 2.0 in 2000.

The lesson that Underwood teaches us is clear. Development policy combined with larger indigenous-based social development strategy will produce better results than development policy based solely on growth and the distribution of social and economic resources. She acknowledges the vehemence of Islamic militancy and anti-Western ideology but reminds us that underneath in Iran were Islamic concepts of social policy consistent with most Western notions of the good.

Why were public authorities so successful in Iran? She argues that it was the fortuitous combination of social vision and political will that was previously absent. No other form of ideology, save socialism, has proven as successful at changing public health practices.

She points out that Muslim peoples, regardless of doctrines, share common mores and connect their public lives with their private ones. If development policies are concordant with Islam, they can be more effective than those policies that are antithetical to Islam.

Implications

What can the reader learn from these essays? Some may learn to acknowledge that there are compelling Islamic principles of family equity that differ from western concepts of individual equality. They might acknowledge that there are widely utilized religious systems of social welfare that can be as effective as welfare organized by the state, and they might recognize the tensions that can arise between the two systems. Some readers may take lessons for the development assistance agencies, which operate, not only in Islamic nations, but in all nations where religious views are important. For too long development assistance agencies have ignored religion in their strategies (Marshall, 2003). It would be wise for them organize economic development objectives around the extant social goals, including those organized by religious authorities.

Notes

1. Five schools of law have been taught at Al-Azhar (university) over the past one thousand years; in addition to the four Sunni schools, there is the Jafari school, which is the major Shi'a sect. Not all Shi'a Muslims are Jafari—only the Twelver Imam Shi'a, the branch of Shi'ism embraced by the majority of Iranians.
2. Westerners might best think of bride-price as being analogous to a prenuptial agreement in which one side (the bridegroom's family)

puts up insurance to guard against the chances of a precipitous and unjustified divorce.

3. Among the more prominent theorists from Egypt was Sayyid Qutb, who has been credited with being the intellectual underpinning for Al-Qaeda (Berman 2003).

4. Pakistan has been a member of the UN, the World Bank, and the IMF since its independence in 1947, but in the half century between independence and the date of Richardson's visit, no description of Pakistan's fiscal affairs covered the administration of zakat or waqf.

Bibliography

Berman, Paul. 2003. "Al Qaeda's Philosopher." *New York Times Magazine*, March 23, 24–30.

Esposito, John L. 1982. *Women in Muslim Family Law*. Syracuse, N.Y.: Syracuse University Press.

Fernea, Elizabeth Warnock. 1998. *In Search of Islamic Feminism*. New York: Doubleday.

Heyneman, Stephen P. 2000. "From the Party/State to Multi-Ethnic Democracy: Education and Social Cohesion in the Europe and Central Asia Region." *Educational Evaluation and Policy Analysis* 22(2): 173–91.

———. 2002–2003. "Defining the Influence of Education on Social Cohesion." *International Journal of Educational Policy, Research, and Practice* 3(4): 73–97.

Mahdavi, Shireen. 1985. "The Position of Women in Shi'a Iran: Views of the 'Ulama." In *Women and the Family in the Middle East*, edited by Elizabeth Warnock Fernea, 255–73. Austin: University of Texas Press.

Marshall, Katherine. 2001. "Development and Religion: A Different Lens on the Development Debate." *Peabody Journal of Education* 76(3–4): 339–75.

Moghadam, Valentine M. 1993. *Modernizing Women: Gender and Social Change in the Middle East*. Boulder, Colo.: Lynne Rienner Publishers.

Mueller, Eric. 1985. "Revitalizing Old Ideas: Developments in Middle Eastern Family Law." In *Women and the Family in the Middle East*, edited by Elizabeth Warnock Fernea, 224–9. Austin: University of Texas Press.

1

The Islamic Institution of Waqf: A Historical Overview[1]

Ahmad Dallal

As mentioned in the introduction, to the extent that all social classes, races, and ethnic groups are treated equally, Islam is a religion of absolute equality. But because inheritance from one generation to the next is carefully prescribed, one can say that Islam also represents a system of wealth redistribution. Essential in any religion, charity is a central organizing principle in Islam. This article examines the organization of charity in Islam.

Although little space is devoted to it in the canonical legal books of the classical period of Islam, the law of *waqf* has emerged as one of the most important branches of Islamic law.

DEFINITION

Waqf[2] (plural *awqaf*) is the only form of perpetuity known in Islam (Makdisi 1981). The Arabic term means withholding or preventing. In Islamic legal terminology waqf means "the detention of the corpus [of a specific property] from the ownership of any person, and the gift of its income [or usufruct] either presently or in the future, to some charitable purpose."[3] In other words, waqf protects something by preventing it from becoming the property of a third person (Othman 1984).

A waqf is a pious endowment established when an owner of a property surrenders his power of disposal of part or all of that property. The founding of a waqf thus means the extinction of the right of property without transferring this right to some other party.[4] Theoretically, therefore, a waqf retains its substance in perpetuity.[5] The founder also surrenders the power of disposal of the returns or the usufruct that the waqf may yield, but he or she has the right to specify the uses of the income from his or her dedicated property on the condition that they fall within the Islamic limit of permitted good. The deed or instrument of a waqf specifies any or all of the following: the uses of the income, the beneficiaries, the priorities of expenditure, the person or persons who will administer the property, and the powers those administrators may have (Heffening 1934).

ORIGINS

The Qur'an has no explicit mention of the concept of waqf. Most Muslim jurists believe that there is no precedence for waqf in pre-Islamic Arabia (Heffening 1934). It has often been argued that the origins of the institution of waqf in Islam are similar, even identical, to those of ancient church property, with collective ownership and use by the religious community (Othman 1983). It has also been argued that Muslims were exposed to the idea of pious endowments in the lands they conquered, where they found Byzantine/Christian foundations that were dedicated for the public benefit and were administered by the bishops (Heffening 1934; Othman 1983).

However, although it is true that the separation of ownership from usufruct was not a new legal concept, the complex Islamic legal system developed to allocate, administer, and dispense this usufruct is entirely Islamic (Cattan 1955, 205). Moreover, the fully developed form of pious endowment in medieval Christianity and medieval Islam differed significantly. The ritualistic and ecclesiastical use of endowments in medieval Christianity and their increasing sacramental orientation are considerably different from the Islamic institution of waqf which has a much broader application and supports a wide variety of life-oriented actions (Jones 1980).

The oldest awqaf, according to Islamic tradition, are the public pious awqaf of K'aba in Mecca and the family waqf of Mashhad al-Khalil in Hebron (the cave of Machpelah in Kirjatharba), both of which are believed to have been founded by the Prophet Abraham about 1860 B.C.E.According to this tradition, Abraham built the K'aba and dedicated it for the worship of God; he also purchased the cave of Machpelah, which remained in his family and where he and Isaac and Jacob and their wives were buried (Othman 1983).

More important than these speculations is the traditional account of the Islamic roots of the waqf institution. The literature of Prophetic Tradition (*hadith*), which is the second authoritative source of legislation in Islam after the Qur'an, preserves recurrent traditions referring to the establishment of a certain mosque waqf by Muhammad.

An even more circulated tradition refers to what is considered the first Islamic land waqf: upon his request, 'Umar (a companion of the Prophet and the second caliph of Islam) is advised by Muhammad to "retain the corpus [of the land of Thamgh, in the region of Khaybar] but dedicate its fruits [in the way of] God." According to this tradition, 'Umar dedicated the land indicating that it should not be sold, given away as a gift, or inherited. He also stipulated that the revenue from the land be used as charity for the poor, for his relatives, for setting slaves free, for wanderers, and for other social needs.[6]

Therefore, hadith literature and the Islamic emphasis on charity give the waqf institution validation. Qur'anic verses and other traditions that are less explicit also support and validate waqf. Such verses include numerous Qur'anic commandments and injunctions that call for good deeds, charity, spending in the way of God, and doing good for relatives.[7] Charity is also considered the way to make provisions in one's lifetime for the continuation of such a practice in the future (Othman 1983). One tradition attributed to Muhammad states that "once a son of Adam dies, none of his deeds will be of use to him except an ongoing charity, a useful knowledge, or a pious child who prays for him." The ongoing charity in this hadith was interpreted to mean waqf (al-Khatib 1968, 46).

Legal Principles

OWNERSHIP

In Islam, the very concept of property involves the idea of its being owned by someone possessed of full powers of disposition over it. Since there exists no Islamic notion of a "legal person" or a collective or institutional subject, it follows that the owner of any property has to be a specified individual (Othman 1984). The general Hanafi definition given above remains silent on the question of ownership, and this led to the first set of legal controversies concerning waqf.

Abu Hanifa argued that the founder of the waqf remains the owner, but loses the rights of selling, bequeathing, or giving away the dedicated property (al-Khatib 1968, 44). If the founder is no longer the owner, Abu Hanifa maintained, then the future usufruct would not go to the beneficiaries, since, at the time of its dedication, it does not constitute an entity that could be given away, and at the time it is actually produced it can not be given away by the founder, who no longer owns it.

The founder's right of ownership continues unless he or she transfers the ownership to a specific individual. Short of such a transfer, the founder can revoke the waqf, sell its subject, or alter its terms at will. Waqf thus becomes, according to this view, a permissible institution that is neither binding nor permanent. It becomes obligatory when the judge sanctions such a move, when words of bequest are used in its constitution, or when a waqf is made in favor of a mosque or burial grounds. In the latter case, the ownership would pass to God, and individuals could have no more rights in it (Othman 1984).

Abu Yusuf and Imam Muhammad (students of Abu Hanifa and major authorities of the Hanafi school) argued that the ownership of the corpus of the waqf belongs to God. Such being the case, the property cannot be sold, given away as a gift, or inherited. Furthermore, the founder's rights are completely extinguished because waqf is analogous to a sale, that is, it is void if made temporarily, and because the implied ownership of the property belongs to God while the ownership of the advantage belongs to the community or to the specified beneficiaries (al-Khatib 1968, 44; Othman 1984).

According to this view, the ownership of the usufruct goes to charity if the beneficiaries become extinct. Similar opinions are also held by Shafi'i and most Shafi'i jurists, although they argue that in this case the usufruct reverts to the founder's heirs. Other Shafi'is, and most Hanbalis, argue that, in the latter case, the waqf remains perpetual, while its income goes first to poor relatives of the founder, then to regular relatives if there are no poor ones, and, finally, to fulfill community interests as the judge deems suitable (Othman 1984).

Some Hanbalis and Shafi'is maintain that the ownership is transferred to the beneficiaries upon establishing a waqf. This ownership, however, is limited or incomplete since the beneficiaries cannot alienate the property; that is, they cannot sell, mortgage, or give it away (al-Khatib 1968, 44).

According to the Maliki school, the waqf may be limited as to time or generation of life. After the expiration of waqf, the ownership reverts back to the founder or the founder's heirs. This indicates that Malikis assume the founder has the real ownership as long as he or she lives and becomes the fictitious owner after death (Othman 1984).

The above differences notwithstanding, according to most schools, the founder's rights of ownership are either lost, or at least radically restricted, as soon as the requirements of a valid waqf are fulfilled. Upon its conclusion, the waqf becomes binding, cannot be revoked, and the founder has no right to alter it (al-Khatib 1968, 56).

WAQF REVENUE

Waqf is classified into two major kinds based on the way its revenue is applied: *waqf Khayri* (charitable endowment) and *waqf ahli* (family waqf) In the first kind the revenue of the waqf is dedicated for the expenses and maintenance of colleges, Sufi lodges, mosques, hospitals, drinking fountains, bridges, waterworks, aqueducts, improving and paving of streets and sidewalks, and for maintaining city walls and other public institutions. Also included under the charitable kind are awqaf dedicated for the maintenance of the holy places in Mecca, Medina, and Jerusalem and paying for the needs of the wayfarers, strangers in transit, widows, orphans, the poor, the aged, and the handicapped, as well as for ransoming prisoners of war, supplying wedding gifts to girls whose families are unable to provide them, and other needs. The family waqf is, as the title indicates, one in which the revenue is dedicated for the descendants of the founder (Rabie 1971; Heffening 1934; Makdisi 1981; Othman 1983).

Since the dedicated property of a waqf is supposed to be perpetual, it then follows that this property should be preserved in continuous repair, so that it will always be in the same condition as it was at the time of dedication. The income of a waqf should thus be applied to the repair and upkeep of the corpus of the waqf, and whatever surplus remains goes to the beneficiaries specified by the founder (Heffening 1934; Othman 1983).

The basic principle applied in the distribution of income from an endowment is that the person who enjoys the profit must also bear the loss (Othman 1983). The inhabitants of a house waqf will pay the repairs of this house since they enjoy its benefits. If, however, they fail to repair it due to neglect, poverty, or unwillingness, then the administrator should obtain an approval from the judge to let the house out. He should then apply the rent to pay for the repairs. When these repairs are completed, the house should be given back to the initial inhabitants for whom the house was dedicated. Thus, the beneficiary of a dedicated house (or a cultivated land) cannot be compelled to fix the house or cultivate the land, even if he or she has the means to do so. The beneficiaries will always have the right to the benefit, though this cannot be at the expense of the corpus itself. Once the property is restored to its initial condition, the rights of the beneficiaries should also be restored. Repair means only preserving the waqf in the state it was in at the time of dedication and does not include improving or developing it (Othman 1983; al-Marghinani 1985).

Numerous legal rulings preserved in various cities and over different periods of time tell of a recurrent problem faced by the waqf foundations: insufficient waqf income (Makdisi 1981). The expenditure of waqf income is determined by a number of variables including the waqf deed (which specifies the wishes of the founder), the upkeep and repair needs of the corpus, and the rights of the beneficiaries.

If the items of expenditure are specified by the founder, his or her will should be followed as much as possible. The rights of the founder include, however, keeping the endowment in good shape, whether this is specifically mentioned in the deed of the waqf or not (Othman 1983; Makdisi 1981). If the income is not sufficient then the first beneficiary in priority is the foundation itself (Makdisi 1981). Income should then be diverted to pay for the most essential administrator(s) needed for running the waqf (Othman 1983), then to pay the salaries of the people whose jobs fulfill the purpose of the waqf, such as the Imam of a mosque, the teachers of a college, and so forth. Here, provision should be made to reduce the number of jobs to the least possible number.

Next, the beneficiaries are classified and ranked either to exclude some or to pay them on a varying scale (Makdisi 1981).

In short, the income should be expended on the objects that are closest and most essential to the general purpose for which the waqf was made. When it is no longer possible to apply the income of waqf on the specified object of the foundation, it should be transferred to another waqf serving as similar an objective as possible (Heffening 1934; Makdisi 1981).

CONDITIONS FOR A LEGITIMATE FOUNDER

To have the right to establish a waqf, the founder must have the full power of disposal over his or her property; that is, one should be mature, of age, sane, free, and in full possession of one's physical and mental powers. The founder should also have unrestricted ownership of the subject to be dedicated (Makdisi 1981; Heffening 1934; al-Khatib 1968, 66). Furthermore, he or she does not have to be a Muslim but can only establish a waqf whose purposes are compatible with Islam.[8]

CONDITIONS ON PROPERTY

To be a valid subject of waqf, the property, at the time of dedication, should be defined, tangible, real, and immobile. The property, therefore, is often made up of some kind of income-yielding real estate (Heffening 1934; Makdisi 1981; al-Khatib 1968, 91; Cattan 1955, 205).

The first question arising concerning the definition of a valid property is its divisibility: if an indefinite part of a property is dedicated as waqf, the dedication is lawful, even if the property in question is indivisible in nature. The property can be divided by applying its income to different purposes at different times or by renting it and dividing the rent. The only exception when no such division or alteration is permissible is in the case of a mosque or a burial ground (al-Marghinani 1985).

Jurists differed on the dedication of property that is mobile.[9]

Whereas Abu Hanifa thought that waqf of movables is altogether unlawful, Abu Yusuf argued that the waqf of items that are dependent on the land is lawful. Such items would include, for example, cattle appropriated with the land to which they belong, as well as horses, camels, and arms dedicated for the Islamic holy war (*jihad*). Another Hanafi jurist, Imam Muhammad, argued that all movables can be made waqf. The remaining legal schools allow (with differences on details) the waqf of movables in the case of things that can be subject to legal agreement such as animals for their milk, trees for their fruits, and so on. The opponents of movable waqf departed from the principle that waqf entails perpetuity, and since movables are not perpetual, then by analogy they too cannot be made waqf.[10] Jurists in favor of the waqf of movables started from the fact that it was common practice to dedicate movable items such as horses for war, or axes and saws with land, and since common practice takes precedence over analogy, these jurists ruled in favor of movable awqaf (Suhrawardy 1911). In short, a majority of jurists argued for the validity of the waqf of movables that are dependent on the dedicated property or are of utility. This validity was based on the common practice of Muslims over the ages.

A major point of legal contention was the question of cash waqf. With the exception of some isolated legal opinions, most authoritative jurists and scholars of classical Islam condemned cash waqf as being equivalent to usury (*riba*), which is strictly forbidden in Islam. Cash, it was also argued, is used for valuation, which means that it changes value over time and has no perpetuity, which is essential in waqf (al-Khatib 1968, 88; Heffening 1934; Suhrawardy 1911, 342). Some time during the fifteenth century, however, cash waqf was legitimized by the Ottoman courts, despite its earlier condemnation. The principles of customary practice and communal benefit, which were used by the Hanafi jurists in the case of the waqf of movables, were also used to justify cash waqf (Suhrawardy 1911, 345, 355–8; Mandaville 1979).

PURPOSE OF WAQF

A waqf should be founded for the purpose of charity and pleasing God. Within the boundaries of this requirement, however, there is room for much flexibility, since charity is not restricted and could easily be applied to the next in kin or members of the family. Moreover, beyond indicating the general purpose of the waqf, the founder may or may not specify the beneficiaries to whom the income should be applied and may defer the application of the charity purposes for as long as a member of the family within the specified beneficiaries exists. Furthermore, with the aid of legal tricks, a waqf whose benefits go to the founder himself or herself can even be established (Heffening 1934; al-Khatib 1968, 96; Makdisi 1981; Mahmood 1972).

THE WAQF CONTRACT

To be valid, a waqf deed should satisfy certain requirements. The founder has to declare orally or, more frequently the case, in writing some object of the waqf. The founder should indicate, in the unambiguous terms of *waqaftu, habastu,* or *sabbaltu,* his or her intention to establish an irrevocable endowment in perpetuity. The founder should indicate for what purpose and in whose favor the endowment is made (Heffening 1934; Makdisi 1981). The declared motive, rather than the intentions of its founder, is the true test of validity of the waqf (Makdisi 1981). As such, the waqf deed provides information on the expectations and hopes of the founder, which may not correspond to the actual way the waqf is developed or used (McChesney 1991, 19).

The waqf cannot be made conditional; that is, a statement such as "I found a waqf if . . ." is not valid (al-Khatib 1968, 67). Moreover, stipulations that contradict the principles of waqf, such as founding a waqf with a stipulation that allows the alienation of its property or with conditions that are opposed to the tenets of Islam, such as a waqf that requires committing sins, are not valid, though the waqf itself may still be so. This means, therefore, that illegal stipulations are dropped, while the waqf itself still holds (al-Khatib 1968, 67 and 71; Makdisi 1981; Suhrawardy 1911, 419).

Waqf, in principle, should be in perpetuity and inalienable; that is, it admits no sale, disposition, mortgage, gift, inheritance, attachment, or so forth (Heffening 1934; Makdisi 1981; Cattan 1955, 207–8). There are some differences, however, on the question of perpetuity: Some jurists maintain that perpetuity is implied by simply using the term waqf, whereas others assume that perpetuity is assured by the inclusion of a charitable element in the waqf, in which case a family waqf with no clear charitable part attached to it is not sufficiently valid.

According to both opinions, the founder does not have to mention the term "perpetuity," since no waqf could be otherwise (Othman 1984). A founder can also bring a legal suit before the court against the administration of the waqf. In such a case, the founder would demand restoring his or her property based on the mismanagement of the waqf, but a final decision on the matter would be left to the judge presiding over the case (Heffening 1934). Of the Islamic schools of law, the Malikis also allow the founder or heirs to revoke the waqf by establishing a waqf with a temporary charter (Heffening 1934; Layish 1983). All schools also agree that the one case when a waqf can be alienated is when it is exchanged for equivalent property or sold on the condition that the proceeds be reinvested in other property (Makdisi 1981).

Aside from the cases when it is illegal, the founder can stipulate a number of conditions regarding the increase or decrease of the wages of employees, the form of administration of the waqf, the uses of revenue and the application of benefits to specific beneficiaries or objects, the situations in which certain beneficiaries are included or excluded, and the preference for allocation of benefits in case of a shortage in the income (Heffening 1934; al-Khatib 1968, 106–16; Layish 1983). Moreover, the founder can stipulate that he or she has the power to alter or modify the conditions of the waqf. This is a one-time right unless the waqf deed clearly stipulates that the founder has the power to repeatedly alter the original deed (al-Khatib 1968, 118 20; Makdisi 1981). The conditions made by the founder, if legal, are equal to the conditions imposed by the law (Othman 1983).

WAQF ADMINISTRATION

The waqf administration includes any number of employees responsible for the disposal, maintenance, treasury, collection, administration, and supervision of a waqf-related operation. Among the titles of some such administrators are *mutawalli*, *wakil*, *nazir*, and *amin* (Makdisi 1981). In addition to the state, which is a party involved in its legal operation, the waqf institution produced over time a full-fledged bureaucracy that continued to evolve and adapt to changing social, economic, and political conditions (McChesney 1991, 14 and 318).

The waqf administrator is usually named by the founder, although the judge retains the right to change the administrator if corrupt and untrustworthy. If the deed does not name an administrator, then the judge assumes the role of trustee and appoints one. If there is no judge, then the trusteeship devolves upon the notables, religious scholars, and the pious of the specific locality in which the waqf is founded. In all events, "no trust should fail for want of trustee," and no waqf should be without supervision or control (Makdisi 1981).

An administrator may engage in any of the following tasks: insure that the original property is preserved and repaired when necessary; rent the property for residence, cultivation, or other purposes; collect the rent or income from cultivation or fruits; develop the property; preserve, regulate, and distribute a fund or an income; take care of the beneficiaries and deal with their problems; arbitrate disputes related to the waqf; insure that the waqf is meeting its designed needs (including the appointment of needed employees); and see to it that the waqf is administered in accordance with the conditions set down in the deed (Othman 1983; Makdisi 1981).

It follows that the administrator should be accountable for the proper management, while the judge, on behalf of the community, supervises the performance of the administrator (Othman 1983; Makdisi 1981). A committee of trustees can also be appointed by the founder to replace the judge in supervising the operation of waqf (Makdisi 1981).

There is disagreement on whether the founder has the right to retain authority over the established waqf. The Malikis, in contrast to most other schools, prohibit the founder from being the administrator of his or her own waqf. The decline in popularity of the Maliki school can be attributed to the fact that it was not appealing to founders of waqf who, in most cases, wanted to maintain some power over their endowments (Makdisi 1981; Layish 1983). The Hanafis, in contrast, maintain that if the founder can give authority to others over the waqf, then the founder should be able to give it to him or herself (al-Marghinani 1985). If, however, the founder turns out to be a person of ill character, then the judge retains the right to discharge him or her in the interest of the public (al-Marghinani 1985; Makdisi 1981).

Finally, the judge represents the community. In the event that the waqf has no income and is falling into ruin, the judge has the power to authorize the administrator to let the building or land temporarily in order to repair it with the proceeds from this rent (Othman 1983). The judge also has the power to authorize the selling of the waqf property if the income is not enough to cover the maintenance. In this case, however, the proceeds should be used to buy another property to be used for the objectives of the old endowment (Othman 1983; Makdisi 1981).

WAQF DISMEMBERMENT AND ALIENATION

Theoretically, a waqf becomes extinct only if its founder secedes from Islam. A number of legal tools were employed over the course of time to reverse certain aspects of waqf that are supposed to be irreversible. Some of these tools amounted to what may be considered tricks to circumvent the law, whereas others were based on more serious revisionist interpretations of the law.

One trick that can be used to invalidate and revoke a waqf is simply for the founder to recede temporarily from Islam, the one act that would lead to the extinction of waqf. The founder would then reclaim his or her Islam, avoiding the penalty of recession (Heffening 1934). This trick is clearly unethical from an Islamic point of view, but it produces the desired effects at a minimal expense during the lifetime of the founder; and since intentions are only judged by God, the punishment of someone who resorts to this trick is postponed to the day of judgment.

Another Shafi'i trick for founding a waqf whose benefit goes back to the founder is to sell a property at a low price to a person who, in turn, makes it a waqf for the original owner (Heffening 1934).

More important than these tricks, however, are the procedures actually used to dismember a waqf and to convert its inalienable property into transferable assets. The first step in this process consists of securing the approval of the local judge that the property in question is either harmful to the public or is a loss to the waqf (Baer 1979). After securing the consent of the judge, a number of methods could be used to alienate the property or parts of its assets:

a) *Istibdal,* for which there are provisions in the law, consists of exchanging the waqf property for a similar and more suitable one, or selling it and applying the money towards buying a new property, to be dedicated for the object of the original waqf (Baer 1979).
b) *Hikr,* introduced in the twelfth century in Egypt and frequently used in Egypt and Syria, grants the tenant of the waqf property a priority of lease, the right of permanent lease, or the perpetual right to the usufruct of the waqf. A lease in perpetuity or for a long period of time (e.g., ninety years) is granted to the tenant in return

for maintaining the property, building on it, or cultivating it (Heffening 1934; Baer 1982). This kind of lease was intended to give the occupant incentive to maintain and develop deteriorated waqf property (Baer 1982). The tenant also has the right to sell the right of perpetual lease, and hikr contracts are inherited according to the Islamic law of inheritance. Finally, the occupant may pay during the long period of lease a rent that changes as the value of the property changes, or, in the case of Maliki law, a fixed rent (Heffening 1934; Baer 1982; al-Khatib 1968, 175–87). Different names are used for similar contracts, thus the terms *inzal* and *nasba* in Tunisia, *muqata'a* in Turkey, and *jalsa* in Morocco (Heffening 1934; Baer 1982).

c) *Ijaratayn* (dual of *ijara*) is a procedure through which tenants can obtain permanent rights to the land. Ijaratayn means two rents, and it differs from the *ijara Tawila* (one extended rent) in that the judge allows letting the property for a long period at a fixed or variable *low* rent. The total rent is then calculated for the duration of the lease period and is divided into two parts: The first part is paid in total at the beginning of the lease, while the second symbolic low rent is paid yearly to insure that the right of ownership does not pass to the tenant. It must be added, however, that, as in the case of hikr, the holder of an ijaratayn contract becomes the effective owner of the waqf property (Heffening 1934; Baer 1979; 1982; al-Khatib 1968, 175–87; Cattan 1955, 209–10). This contract was common in Anatolia in the sixteenth and seventeenth centuries.

d) *Khulu* is a contract commonly used in Egypt, Tunisia, and Syria as early as the sixteenth century. In this contract, the tenant repairs the property, and the expenditure becomes a claim in the tenant's favor on the waqf. This gives the tenant some rights to the property itself in addition to a long-term lease for a fixed low rent. A khulu can be reversed if the administrator of the waqf can somehow pay its debt (Baer 1979; 1982). Although a procedure such as the khulu contract is designed to free property and to make it alienable, the actual practice in many of the cases in which it was employed was to dedicate the newly appropriated rights to new awqaf; thus waqf was often regenerated rather than mobilized in what seems to be a drive to create room to new comers to participate in the waqf system rather than to abolish the system itself (Roded 1988, 90–1).

APPLICATIONS AND USES OF WAQF

The essential use of waqf was to provide for a certain amount of the public expenses and to perform many of the services that are the responsibility of the public sector in the modern state. In addition, waqf systems duplicate many of the roles played in the modern states by public, nontrading corporations, religious and charitable foundations and trusts, religious offices, and family settlements (Makdisi 1981).

The subjects of waqf included such properties as agricultural land, gardens, farms, and even whole villages, as well as shops, warehouses, hotels, stables, houses, apartment buildings, baths, mills, bakeries, oil and sugar presses, soap works, paper works, looms, and post houses. The proceeds from the dedicated property should be expended on the object of the waqf, and only the money needed to repair the basic corpus could be spent on the waqf itself. Moreover, there are no fees to pay in a waqf charitable trust, and no proceeds could be added to the basic waqf in order to enlarge the endowment (Makdisi 1981).

The result is an institution that has a permanent nature from a legal point of view but has no built-in mechanisms to replenish itself, which gives rise to the need for periodic infusion of investment into an existing waqf to ensure its longevity. This is secured through the introduction of new capital investments from outside and independent sources, transformation of the original uses of the waqf into more efficient and lucrative ones, finding sources of new income, establishing new auxiliary endowments, finding ways of securing tax exemptions for the waqf income, protecting of waqf from natural deterioration and from encroachment by the dominant powers, and ensuring efficient and skillful management of the endowment (McChesney 1991, 14 and 318–9).

In historical application, however, waqf has been used for more than charity and supporting the public sector. One obvious use of waqf was to evade the law, either by escaping taxation or, more importantly, by circumventing the Islamic law of inheritance

(Makdisi 1981). The Islamic law of inheritance strictly specifies the heirs and their respective shares, and waqf was one accessible way of favoring one heir over another, establishing equal division of shares between sons and daughters, or favoring the son at the expense of the daughter. In all these cases, Qur'anic heirs are excluded from getting their legal shares (Makdisi 1981; Powers 1989; Layish 1983). It is not clear at this point whether more cases of waqf were used to favor the male or the female heirs. It is certain, however, that many women established waqf to protect their property against the interference and control of their husbands or male members of their families.[11] Of all the awqaf established in the Ottoman period, almost 40 percent were founded by women; in seventeenth- and eighteenth-century Cairo, the number was 30 percent to 40 percent, and similar numbers are recorded for several other case studies. It is even argued that, through waqf establishment, women played an active role in the economic life of their societies (Crecelius 1986).

Another use of waqf is to avoid the division of property due to the breakup that results from applying the Islamic law of inheritance. The inheritance law tends to fragment the property into large numbers of small shares, whereas waqf tends to preserve large amounts of wealth and allows the concentration of property within a line of direct descendants, to the exclusion of collateral, ascendant, and more distant relatives. It thus follows that waqf allows for the transmission of property in viable economic units (Powers 1989).

Aside from the direct economic purposes, the establishment of waqf was intimately related to political conditions and aspirations. Periods of political uncertainty usually witnessed an increased establishment of waqf to protect property from the possible confiscation of emerging political powers (Makdisi 1981; Powers 1989). Positive political ambitions were also fostered through this institution. Establishing a college waqf in favor of a certain school of law may have secured the support of the appointed professors and their followers, in addition to the gratitude, prestige, and power that the founder derived from his or her patronage (Makdisi 1981). In this respect, the prestige of the waqf institution was used as a political bargaining chip (McChesney 1991).

At the ideological level, waqf provided a class of religious notables and scholars (*'ulama*) with an economic base independent of the political authorities (Makdisi 1981). The colleges, mosque-schools, and Sufi lodges sponsored by waqf assured the survival of this class of scholars who were in charge of transmitting the Islamic values and ensuring the harmony and distinctive ideology of the Islamic community (Powers 1989).

Alternatively, waqf was used by central authorities to influence local politics.[12] It was also used to bring about cultural integration by bringing the culture of the central state, as well as public services and security, to the different provinces (McChesney 1981). The Ottoman policy of settlement and expansion, for example, relied heavily on the establishment of awqaf in support of Sufi monasteries that were planted along the frontiers of the expanding empire, on its strategic trade routes and traffic arteries, amidst its political rivals and enemies, or in other strategic locations. In addition, more incentives were given for the settlers in the form of tax waivers and other economic privileges and immunities.[13]

Waqf was also used in urban revitalization projects. Through waqf, agricultural revenues (including rural taxes) were channeled into urban services (McChesney 1981). Major portions of the state revenues were also invested in waqf to support urban institutions, which in turn attracted other smaller businesses and services. New life was injected into cities by reviving their business districts. In one typical case, an endowed cathedral mosque was established that drew people in its direction; a market waqf was then founded next to the mosque, so that people going to pray would pass through the new market, generating customer traffic and economic activity. This arrangement led to the shifting of the city's economic center to the newly created neighborhood

(McChesney 1981). This is a stark example of the use of waqf in the reorganization and development of urban space.[14]

Though not the only factor, the waqf institution was one of the major elements determining the emergence of urban elites and family notables in major Islamic cities. It was used as a legal device for consolidating and enhancing hereditary family power and economic resources.[15]

The uses of waqf mentioned so far can all be legitimately justified. There existed, however, many cases where waqf, and waqf-related contracts, were abused or used for illegitimate ends. It was not uncommon for public officials, for example, to establish waqf on land that belonged to someone else, especially on public property. It also was not uncommon for such officials to confiscate waqf land or seize their revenues. Corrupt administrators were also known to abuse the income of waqf in patterns similar to corrupt bureaucracies in all places and times (Makdisi 1981; Mandaville 1979).

The medieval historian al-Maqrizi, for example, tells of beneficiaries who registered in the name of ruined mosques in Mamluk, Egypt, and of judges who accepted bribes to sell buildings of waqf under the pretext that they were ruined, without using the proceeds to buy new property. He also mentions a certain Mamluk lord of the fourteenth century who, were it not for the adamant opposition of the jurists, almost succeeded in confiscating the waqf property in all of Egypt (cited in Heffening 1934).

Hikr contracts were also used to serve illegitimate ends. To start with, even a legal hikr can be seen as a way of encroaching on waqf property. Once established, it was only a matter of time before many waqf administrators neglected collecting the low rents, in which case the ownership of the property passed to the lessee. Even usurpers claimed such entitlement to ownership. Moreover, dishonest administrators facilitated illegal transfer of ownership (Baer 1982).

Hikr was also used by owners to avoid paying their creditors. An owner in debt could sell the corpus of his property to a mosque at a nominal price on the condition that he could retain the rights to administer, transfer, and enjoy the benefits from this endowed land. In return, he would pay an annual rent equal to the interest on the price originally paid by the mosque. The creditors can thus make no claim on the property itself, while the owner retains virtually full control over it (Baer 1982).

In addition to these abuses, waqf often suffered from the same ills that inflict any welfare system, in which large sections of the community are supported by the public treasury. Moreover, the fact that waqf property is not market controlled, cannot be burdened with mortgage, and cannot be freely exploited deprives it from the benefits of competition and accounts for the lack of incentive among tenants, two factors essential for the development of any property. Waqf property, according to this argument, would thus lie under the "dead hand."[16]

The above argument, though true in some cases, is in no way universally applicable. In actual historical practice, waqf institutions played such varying, and in most cases extremely important, roles in the economic, social, and political development of Islamic societies that no such monolithic statements can be meaningfully substantiated. To obtain insights into the complexity and flexibility of this institution, it is useful to examine the historical record.

Historical Development

The standards set by the Islamic law provide prescriptions and prohibitions on the founding and application of waqf. The particular political and economic conditions, however, delimit the patterns of the real functioning of these regulations (McChesney 1991, 18). The ways waqf functioned in the context of the general regulations set by Islamic law (which varies among the schools) differed from place to place and as a result of the varying needs of the time.

For example, although the dedication of land waqf was known as early as the eighth century in Iraq, most of the early awqaf in Egypt were buildings, whereas the earliest land waqf dates from 930 (Rabie 1971). In tenth-century Fatimid Egypt, the first-known attempts by the state to control waqf were undertaken. Records indicate that, four centuries later under the Mamluks, extensive estates had been constituted as waqf, and the agricultural land waqf in the year 1339 was estimated at 130,000 *feddans* (Heffening 1934; Crecelius 1971). This shows that the law, which allows for the establishment of different kinds of waqf, was exploited in varying degrees depending on the social, economic, and political configurations of the time and place.

Studies of waqf in the social and historical contexts are numerous but not comprehensive, and they do not allow for charting the overall course of development of the institution. Several case studies, however, have focused on the development of the institution of waqf in the Ottoman Empire, and they clearly illustrate the essential role played by waqf at all the historical stages of social and political development. Waqf was instrumental to the conquest and colonization policies of the Ottomans (Layish 1987).

Waqf was also extensively used for the development of public and commercial institutions leading to the economic revitalization of major Ottoman cities, including the rebuilding of Istanbul in the fifteenth century (McChesney 1981, 165; Barnes 1987). In 1527, for example, 12 percent of the whole state revenues were controlled by the waqf administration (McChesney 1981). Waqf was also used as perhaps the major tool for bringing Ottoman culture and services to the conquered regions.[17] During the early period of Ottoman expansion, half the population of several major Ottoman cities were fed by the state.[18] In the seventeenth century, the Sultanic waqf was the principle provider of municipal services in all the major Ottoman cities, in addition to its role as a vehicle for channeling agricultural revenues into urban services (McChesney 1981). The strength of the waqf institution increased to such a level that, by the eighteenth century, the best arable land in the empire was constituted as waqf by the military and civil aristocracy, religious scholars, and members of the Sufi orders (Powers 1989).

In the Ottoman provinces, waqf was also instrumental in bringing about state policies. It was used to influence local politics and to strengthen contenders for local power in the interest of the central state.[19] Furthermore, the use of waqf as a mechanism for deriving political power and social prestige and the participation of centrally appointed Ottoman officials and the local notables in this power dynamic helped bridge the gaps between central and provincial notables and produced a rather homogeneous urban elite throughout the empire.[20]

Investing in waqf was also directly linked to state policy; in eighteenth-century Egypt, the Ottoman administration lowered the taxes on agricultural waqf, leading to an explosion in waqf investment. By the end of the century, one-fifth of the arable land of the country was endowed (Baer 1969, 79; 1962).

An important development in the Ottoman Empire was the introduction of cash waqf, which opened the money market for small lenders and buyers and increased the credit availability in the country.[21] This practice was in opposition to Islamic law and was justified (though not convincingly) on the basis of common practice. Aside from the opposition of major jurists based on normative Islamic discourse, it is possible to come out with different assessments concerning this kind of waqf. It can be argued that the introduction of cash waqf provided more financial opportunities for a larger number of small investors. This activity, however, led to an expansion of cash waqf to the point that, by the year 1560, the amount of cash waqf exceeded the non-cash kind, and the cash waqf was invested mainly in loans to peasants. The resulting large amount of peasant indebtedness may account for the endemic peasant insurrections between 1580 and 1650 (Mandaville 1979).

A similar study tracing the development of a waqf in Shi'i, Safavid Iran, between 1480 and 1889, confirms the importance of examining the development of waqf in its historical context and exposes the ways in which the institution is intertwined with, and influenced by, the different facets of social reality (McChesney 1991).

It is clear that the merits of different reforms can only be appreciated in the context of their specific histories and not in light of later notions of legal or economic reform. The importance of this observation is accentuated by two extreme positions held by scholars of Islamic law. At one extreme, some argue that legal reform was only brought about as a result of Western modernization that opened the Islamic legal code to modern interpretations.[22] The developments in the Ottoman Empire (and elsewhere), which included attempts to codify the law of waqf (and other laws), the use of hikr contracts to alienate waqf land, and the introduction of cash waqf, point to the flexibility and potential for development of the waqf legal package; these developments were resorted to long before the westernization of Islamic countries. At the other extreme, some scholars argue that these reforms are symptomatic of legal decadence (Mandaville 1979), yet the many examples listed above of the positive and constructive use of the legal reform of waqf suggest that, at least in a great number of cases, such reforms cannot be so simply dismissed.

WAQF IN MODERN TIMES

The nineteenth and twentieth centuries witnessed major developments in the status and laws of waqf in Islamic countries. The colonial experience and the emergence of modern nation-states radically redefined some of the major features of the institution. After recurrent conflicts between newly imposed legal codes and the traditional laws of waqf, a series of changes were introduced, ranging from regulating to completely abolishing waqf. All such measures were justified in the contexts of legal and economic reforms. As a result of those developments, family waqf was abolished in most Islamic countries while the public charitable waqf was brought under the stringent control of the state.

The issue of waqf was raised in several modern encounters between the age-old institution and colonial powers and, later, the rising nation-states. These encounters can be distinguished from earlier reforms in that they questioned the viability of the waqf institution and sought to limit or even abolish it.

After their occupation of Algeria, the French authorities gradually and systematically replaced the Islamic law with French public, property, and penal law. Islamic law was then restricted to the realm of personal status, including marriage, divorce, and inheritance. However, while French authorities considered waqf subject to the French law of property, Muslims considered it part of the law of succession and subject to Islamic jurisdiction.

A heated legal debate ensued in which French jurists were divided. In 1874, the Court of Algiers finally validated the opinion that family waqf was a special case of the Islamic law of inheritance. This legislative enactment, however, was inadequate for the French colonizers, whose desires to buy Algerian land were frustrated by the inalienability of most of the useful agricultural land. A large number of French Orientalists embarked on an attempt to redefine Islamic law, a main purpose being to discredit and delegitimize the Islamic law of waqf.

The outcome of this attempt was to distinguish between family waqf and public waqf and to accuse the former of retarding the social and economic development of the nation by immobilizing large sections of its capital resources. Furthermore, French Orientalists, presenting themselves as advocates of Islamic ethics, even informed Muslims that family waqf violates Islamic inheritance law and was not valid from an Islamic point of view.[23] Although completely baseless, the French view on waqf remains the dominant view in modern scholarship on this subject, and it accounts for the notion that the waqf institution, particularly family waqf, is neither viable in modern times nor compatible with Islamic legal norms.

In contrast to their French counterparts, the British in India assumed a positive posture toward Islamic law in general, and they codified Islamic law, subject to major alterations, in what came to be known as the Anglo-Muhammedan Law. Cases of conflict did arise, however, when Hindu creditors made claims on properties already endowed by the debtors. After a series of rulings (in favor of the creditors) and appeals (by the heirs of the debtors), a case was brought in 1894 before the Privy Council, the highest legal body in the British Empire, which declared family waqf invalid. A major wave of opposition by Muslim lawyers and religious scholars culminated in the Waqf Validating Act, which led, in 1913, to the full restoration and validation of the judicial enforceability of family awqaf in India. Pakistan, Bangladesh, and Burma inherited the 1913 Act of India, which, with some modifications, is still valid today.[24]

In the post-1952 period, several Arab countries moved to abolish family waqf or at least to considerably restrict it. Charitable waqf, on the other hand, was brought under the control of either a ministry or a department of awqaf. In Egypt, Syria, Tunisia, and Libya, for example, the argument for this change was that waqf laws were *ijtihadi* laws (i.e., they were based on speculative reasoning and not the clear-cut injunctions of the scripture), and it was up to the state to review them based on the needs of the society. In so arguing, religious and secular reformers resurrected the views produced at the turn of the century by French Orientalists, with little, if any, regard for the actual historical record.[25]

However, despite the reduction in its influence in the social and political spheres, and despite the considerable reduction in the size of its properties and revenues, waqf remains an institution of substantial wealth and potential, and it still retains some

of the historical flexibility that qualifies it to play a major role in
the life of Islamic societies.

Notes

1. For a discussion of ways in which a contemporary state, Pakistan,
   tried to incorporate the traditional notion of waqf into a ministry,
   see the section on waqf in chapter 6.
2. The term used in North Africa, as well as in many Islamic legal works
   is *habus* (French habous.)
3. This is the standard definition in the Hanafi legal school that one
   would find in most primary sources; see al-Khatib 1968, 43; and
   Cattan 1955, 203. In addition to the Shi'i legal school there are four
   Sunni legal schools in Islam, namely Maliki, Hanafi, Shafi'i, and
   Hanbali.
4. For definitions see al-Marghinani 1985 and Heffening 1934.
5. Pending, of course, on proper maintenance of the substance of the
   waqf.
6. The two traditions appear in the two most authenticated collections
   of hadith, namely Bukhari and Muslim; see, for example, references
   in Heffening 1934 and Othman 1983.
7. See, for example, al-Khatib 1968, 46.
8. For a sample waqf instrument for a foundation established in the
   Ottoman period by a Maronite for the education of the members of
   his sect see Ebied and Young 1975.
9. On the waqf of movables see Heffening 1934; al-Marghinani 1985;
   and Suhrawardy 1911.
10. The point of departure for the opponents of movable waqf was the
    principle that waqf entail perpetuity, and since movables are not
    perpetual, then by analogy they too cannot be made waqf.
11. On women and waqf see Baer 1983.
12. For an example from eighteenth-century Jerusalem see Peri 1983.
13. Instances of such policies occurred in Anatolia, Palestine, Libya, and
    the Sudan; see Layish 1987.
14. On the use of waqf for promoting urban policies see McChesney
    1981; Gerber 1983; Peri 1983; Baer 1986; and Roded 1988.
15. On waqf and the urban elites see Baer 1979 and 1986 and Roded
    1988, 87.
16. See, for example, Heffening 1934.

17. See McChesney 1981, 165; Layish 1987; and Barnes 1987. Also for a case study of the operation of a medium-sized Ottoman waqf, see Faroqhi 1974.
18. See, for example, the study on waqf in Edrine in Gerber 1983.
19. For the use of waqf as a policy tool in eighteenth-century Ottoman Jerusalem, see Peri 1983.
20. See a study on waqf and social elites in eighteenth-century Aleppo, see Roded 1988.
21. For a discussion of cash waqf in the Ottoman Empire, see Mandaville 1979.
22. See, for example, Coulson 1978, also cited in Mandaville 1979.
23. On waqf controversies in French Algeria, see Mahmood 1988; Powers 1989; Anderson 1952, 257–76; and Christelow 1985. For writings by French Orientalists on waqf see Sautayra 1873–1874; and Mercier 1899.
24. On the waqf controversy in British India see Mahmood 1988; Powers 1989; Kozlowski 1988; Ahmad 1986; and Anderson 1965. For yet another instance of conflict between the interests of occupiers and waqf see the studies on waqf in Israel by Layish 1983; Eisenman 1978; and Tibawi 1978.
25. See, for example, Mahmood 1988 and Baer 1958.

Bibliography

Aberra, Yassin M. 1983–1984. "Muslim Institutions in Ethiopia: The Asmara Awqaf." *Journal of the Institute of Muslim Minority Affairs* 5(1): 203–23.

Ahmad, Furqan. 1986. "Background of the Mussalman Wakf Validating Act, 1913: Shibli Nu'mani's Contribution." *Islamic and Comparative Law Quarterly* 6(2–3): 191–8.

Anderson, J. N. D. 1952. "Recent Development in Shari'a Law IX." *Muslim World* 42: 257–76.

———. 1959. "*Waqfs* in East Africa." *Journal of African Law* 3(3): 3, 152–64.

———. 1965. "A Recent Decision of the Judicial Committee of the Privy Council." In *Arabic and Islamic Studies in Honor of Hamilton A. R. Gibb*, edited by George Makdisi, 53–63. Cambridge: Department of Near Eastern Languages and Literatures of Harvard University, distributed by Harvard University Press.

———. 1970. *Islamic Law in Africa*. London: Cass.

Anderson, Norman. 1976. *Law Reform in the Muslim World*. London: Athlone Press.

Baer, Gabriel. 1958. "*Waqf* Reform in Egypt." *St Antony's Papers* 4: 61–76.

———. 1962. *A History of Landownership in Modern Egypt, 1800–1950*. London: Oxford University Press.

———. 1969. *Studies in the Social History of Modern Egypt*. Chicago: University of Chicago Press.

———. 1979. "The Dismemberment of Awqaf in Early 19th century Jerusalem." *Asian and African Studies* 13(3): 220–41.

———. 1982. "Hikr." In *Encyclopaedia of Islam*, New Edition, supplement, 368–70. Leiden.

———. 1983. "Women and *Waqf*: An Analysis of the Istanbul Tahrir of 1546." *Asian and African Studies* 17(1): 9–27.

———. 1986. "Jerusalem's Families of Notables and the Wakf in the Early 19th century." In *Palestine in the Late Ottoman Period*, edited by David Kushner, 109–22. Jerusalem: Yad Izhak Ben-Zvi; Leiden: Distributed by E. J. Brill.

———. 1997. "The *Waqf* as a Prop for the Social System (Sixteenth-Twentieth Centuries)." *Islamic Law and Society* 4(3): 264–97.

Behrens-Abouseif, D. 1998. "Qaytbay's Investments in the City of Cairo: *Waqf* and Power." *Annales Islamologiques* 32: 29–40.

Barnes, John Robert. 1987. *An Introduction to Religious Foundations in the Ottoman Empire*. Leiden: E. J. Brill.

Bashir, Muhammad. 1977. *The Manual of Auqaf Laws*. Lahore: Law Book Service.

al-Basri, Hilal bin Yahya bin Salama al-Ra'i (Hanafi, d. 859). 1936. *Kitab Ahkam al-Waqf*. Hayderabad: Matba'at Majlis Da'irat al-Ma'arif al-'Uthmaniyah.

Cannon, Byron D. 1982. "The Beylical Habus Council and Suburban Development: Tunis, 1881–1914." *Maghreb Review* 7(1–2): 32–40.

Cattan, Henry. 1955. "The Law of *Waqf*." In *Law in the Middle East*, edited by Majid Khadduri and Herbert J. Liebesny, 203–22. Washington.

Christelow, Allan. 1985. *Muslim Law Courts and the French Colonial State in Algeria*. Princeton, N.J.: Princeton University Press.

Coulson, N. J. 1978. *A History of Islamic Law*. Edinburgh: University Press.

Crecelius, Daniel. 1971. "The Organization of *Waqf* Documents in Cairo." *International Journal of Middle East Studies* 2: 266–77.

———. 1986. "Incidences of *Waqf* Cases In Three Cairo Courts: 1640–

1802." *Journal of the Economic and Social History of the Orient* 29: 176–89.

Ebied, R. Y., and M. J. L. Young, eds. and trans. 1975. *Some Arabic Legal Documents of the Ottoman Period*. Leiden, Netherlands: E. J. Brill.

Eisenman, Robert H. 1978. *Islamic Law in Palestine and Israel*. Leiden, Netherlands: Brill.

Faroqhi, Suraiya. 1974. "Vakif Administration in Sixteenth-Century Konya." *Journal of the Economic and Social History of the Orient* 17(2): 145–72.

Fay, M. A. 1997a. "Women and *Waqf*: Toward a Reconsideration of Women's Place in the Mamluk Household." *International Journal of Middle East Studies* 29(1): 33–51.

———. 1997b. "Women and *Waqf*; Property, Power, and the Domain of Gender in Eighteenth-century Egypt." In *Women in the Ottoman Empire: Middle Eastern Women in the Early Modern Era*, edited by M. C. Zilfi, 28–47. Leiden: Brill.

Gerber, Haim. 1983. "The *Waqf* Institution in Early Ottoman Edrine." *Asian and African Studies* 17(1): 29–45.

Heffening, W. 1934. "Wakf." In *Encyclopaedia of Islam*, First Edition, vol. 4, 1096–1103. Leiden.

Hoexter, M. 1998a. *Endowments, Rulers and Community: Waqf ql-Haramayn in Ottoman Algiers*. Leiden: Brill.

———. 1998b. "*Waqf* Studies in the Twentieth century: The State of the Art." *Journal of the Economic and Social History of the Orient* 41(4): 474–95.

Jones, William R. 1980. "Pious Endowments in Medieval Christianity and Islam." *Diogenes* 109: 23–36.

al-Khassaf, Ahmad bin 'Umar al-Shaybani (Hanafi, d. 875). 1904. *Kitab Ahkam al-Waqf*. Cairo.

al-Khatib, Ahmad 'Ali. 1968. *Al-Waqf wal-Wasaya*. Baghdad.

Kozlowski, Gregory C. 1985. *Muslim Endowment and Society in British India*. Cambridge.

Kozlowski, Gregory C. 1988. "British Judges, Muslim Law and Contemporary Perspectives on Muslim Endowments in South Asia." *Hamdard Islamicus* 11(3): 3–16.

Layish, Aharon. 1966. "The Muslim *Waqf* in Israel." *Asian and African Studies* 2: 41–76.

———. 1983. "The Maliki Family *Waqf* According to Wills and *Waqfiyyat*." *Bulletin of the School of Oriental and African Studies* 46(1): 1–32.

———. 1987. "*Waqfs* and Sufi Monasteries in the Ottoman Policy of

Colonization: Sultan Selim I's *Waqf* in Favour of Dayr al-Asad." *Bulletin of the School of Oriental and African Studies* 50(1): 61–89.

Mahmood, Tahir. 1972. *Islamic Law in Modern India*. Bombay: N. M. Tripathi.

———. 1988 "Islamic Family *Waqf* in Twentieth century Legislation: A Comparative Perspective." *Islamic and Comparative Law Quarterly* 8(1): 1–19.

Makdisi, George. 1981. "The Law of *Waqf*." In *The Rise of Colleges: Institutions of Learning in Islam and the West*, by George Makdisi, 35–74. Edinburgh: Edinburgh University Press.

Mandaville, Jon E. 1979. "Usurious Piety: The Cash *Waqf* Controversy in the Ottoman Empire." *International Journal of Middle East Studies* 10: 289–308.

al-Maqdisi, Ibn Qudama (Hanbali, d. 1000). 1963. *Kitab al-Kafi*. 2 vols. Damascus.

al-Marghinani, Burhan al-Din 'Ali. 1985. "Wakf, or Appropriations." In *Hedaya, or Guide: A Commentary on the Mussulman Laws*, Translated by Charles Hamilton, 334–359. Reprint of 1870 edition. New Dehli, India.

McChesney, Robert D. 1981. "*Waqf* and Public Policy: The *Waqf*s of Shah 'Abbas, 1011–1023/1602–1614." *Asian and African Studies* 15(2): 165–90.

McChesney, Robert D. 1991. *Waqf in Central Asia: Four Hundred Years in the History of a Muslim Shrine, 1480–1889*. Princeton, N.J.: Princeton University Press.

Mercier, Ernest. 1899. *Le code de habous ou ouakf selon la Legislation Musulmane*. Constantine: Imprimerie D. Braham.

Meriwether, M. L. 1997. "Women and *Waqf* Revisited: The Case of Aleppo, 1770–1840." In *Women in the Ottoman Empire: Middle Eastern Women in the Early Modern Era*, edited by M. C. Zilfi, 128–152. Leiden: Brill.

O'Fahey, R. S., and K. S. Vikor. 1996–1997. "A Zanzibar *Waqf* of Books: The Library of the Mundhiri Family." *Sudanic Africa* 7: 5–23.

Othman, Muhammad Zain bin Haji. 1983. "Origins of the Institution of *Waqf*." *Hamdard Islamicus* 6(2): 3–23.

———. 1984. "Istitution of *Waqf*." *Islamic Culture* 58(1): 55–62.

Pearl, David. 1987, *A Textbook on Muslim Personal Law*. London: Croom Helm.

Peri. Oded. 1983. "The *Waqf* as an instrument to Increase and Consolidate

Political Power: The Case of Khasseki Sultan *Waqf* in Late Eighteenth-century Ottoman Jerusalem." *Asian and African Studies* 17(1): 47–62.

Petry, C. F. 1998. "A Geniza for Mamluk Studies? Charitable Trust (*waqf*) Documents as a Source for Economic and Social History." *Mamluk Studies Review* 2: 51–60.

Powers, David S. 1989. "Orientalism, Colonialism, and Legal History: The Attack on Muslim Family Endowments in Algeria and India." *Comparative Studies in Society and History* 31(3): 535–71.

Rabie, Hassanein. 1971. "Some Financial Aspects of the *Waqf* System in Medieval Egypt." *Egyptian Historical Review* 18: 1–24.

Roded, Ruth. 1988. "The *Waqf* and the Social Elite of Aleppo in the Eighteenth and Nineteenth Centuries." *Turcica: Revue des Etudes Turques* 20: 71–91.

———. 1989. "Charities (*Waqfs*) in Turkish Life: Past and Present." *Turkish Review* 3(17): 71–90.

Sautayra, Edouard, and Eugene Cherbonneau. 1873–1874. *Droit musulman: du statut personnel et des successions.* 2 vols. Paris: Maisonneuve et cie.

al-Shafi'i, Muhammad bin Idris (d. 820). n.d. *Kitab al-'Umm.* Vol. 2, part 4. Dar al-Ma'rifa.

Suhrawardy, Al-Ma'mun. 1911. "The *Waqf* of Movables." *Journal and Proceedings of the Asiatic Society of Bengal* 7(6): 323–430.

al-Tanukhi, Sahnun bin Sa'id (Maliki, d. 855). n.d. *Al-Mudawwana al-Kubra.* Vol. 6. Beirut.

al-Tarabulsi, Ibrahim bin Musa bin Abi Bakr al-Shaykh 'Ali (Hanafi, d. 1516). 1952. *Kitab al-Is'af fi Ahkam al-Waqf.* Cairo.

Tibawi, A. L. 1978. *The Islamic Pious Foundations in Jerusalem.* London: Islamic Cultural Centre.

2

Islamic Law and the Position of Women

Donna Lee Bowen

The question of women's status is one of the most sensitive areas in contemporary Islam. Asymmetry between men and women traditionally has been an integral part of Islam and has emerged as a dynamic social issue in the twentieth century. The Islamic world does not face this tension on gender issues alone; non-Muslim cultures face equally difficult choices.

First, if women and men are equal, should not access to resources be allocated equally among them? This would involve a far-reaching redistribution of property and would occasion equal access to work, education, credit, and capital; equal pay; and equal legal rights. Reallocating resources more equitably involves numerous economic and political questions that would engender considerable conflict.

Second, women's place in society and religious or legal support for their status has great symbolic import. These issues bring up subsidiary questions on the roles that men and women hold and their relations with each other, which include primary assumptions about community organization. For conservative religious groups (including Muslim activists), women's behavior has become shorthand for the health of a society. Moreover, women's roles have become a mark of piety and religiosity. Men's religiosity is judged by the demeanor of their women and the women's conformity to ideal norms of behavior. The well-being of the community hinges upon visible patterns of female conduct.

Third, conflict between the Muslim world and the West is at a high point. Not just Muslim activists, but numerous political and social groups, take on legitimacy by defining themselves in opposition to the West. Since women's liberation is perceived as a Western phenomenon and many of the reforms are modeled on Western paradigms, the two are tightly interwoven in the minds of the opponents to change in women's roles. Muslim activists judge women's rights and women's participation in the public sphere to be signs of westernization, not modernization, and therefore a destructive force in society, not a positive turn of events.

Feelings run so high at times that even discussing these issues in any forum can prove arduous. Women's status engenders a great diversity of opinion, and the issues involved are numerous and thorny. This touchiness stems from women's status being closely linked to how each of us defines our personal roles and way of life. No person approaches women's status and roles neutrally. Personal assumptions of what should be can skew our reading of gender issues.

In addition, the position taken as to the status of women generally indicates an individual's viewpoint, be it religious or secular, patriarchal or egalitarian. Thus it is difficult to discuss aspects of this topic dispassionately because so much baggage is attached to the subject.

PURPOSE OF THIS ESSAY

To clarify this complex scene, this essay presents a spectrum of Muslim views on women to differentiate among varied trains of thought and to show points of articulation. Development experts work in all parts of the Muslim world—the Middle East, North Africa, East and West Africa, South Asia, Southeast Asia—where they confront expectations for Muslim women and encounter everyday actions of women—what they say and what they do—that may confound stereotypic beliefs prevalent about Muslim women. This essay surveys precepts of Islamic law to determine how they are used to formulate legal stances on women's issues and reforms of those positions. Here customary practice and expectations often intersect with the historical tenets of a revealed religion. Practice and expectations emphasize women's submissiveness. The Qur'an nowhere states that women submit to male domination and enjoins both men and women to behave judiciously.

Anyone who deals with Islamic law faces the question of the interpretation of Islam and the formulation of Islamic law. Conservatives, reformers, and activists contend for the right to interpret Islam definitively, so any interpretation becomes problematic. Debates on the direction in which society should move still rage between fundamentalists, liberal democrats, leftists, and traditional social groups. In the midst of this struggle, the question of women's role takes prominence. Reasons for this are many.

First, the family is the basic institution of society: its health reflects that of society in general, and women are still seen as the prime keepers of family well-being. Women's roles, in many cultures, are used as symbols that indicate domestic and social order or disorder. Any confusion in that order has society-wide reverberations. Second, defining women's roles also defines men's roles, and societies around the world have been highly resistant to suggestions of gender-role changes. Third, women's issues are highly visible and arouse, as referred to above, considerable emotion and thus are a good rallying point for social movements— conservative or liberal. While the status of women is the major issue, other social and economic issues that are less amenable to symbolic representation lurk in the background as an important, if unstated, part of the overall debate.

This is easily demonstrable in the case of Muslim activism. Various authors have noted that while the role of women is argued and questions such as the veiling of women are publicized, often the real questions are political and economic. Women's issues may symbolize political or economic concerns, or they may be a smokescreen, but they are symbols to which groups readily respond. Women's issues have great weight by themselves but also assume extraordinary significance by being used as a rallying point by those with a separate agenda (Mernissi 1987; Kandiyoti 1991a; 1991b; Keddie 1991; Beck and Keddie 1978; Fernea 1985).

The test comes in a microexamination of family roles. In Muslim society, there has always been a tension between theory and practice. In theory, Muslim women are submissive and dominated by their menfolk; in reality, many are strong, outspoken women who take an active role in their family and community. In theory, Muslim women are well cared for by their spouse and male kin; in practice, many women, unfortunately, are orphaned, widowed, barren, or mistreated and fall through the safety net set up by Islamic law. As in all religious communities, normative prescriptions do not spell reality. Actions of individual Muslims often differ from religious principles. Indeed, these deviations spurred the reforms in Islamic law.

An underlying question on women's status is the equity of social roles: Are women unjustly treated? In Islamic legal texts, are men and women guaranteed equal rights? If not equal, are their rights equitable, and does a coherent argument for equity exist? Definite answers are difficult, for it depends on which group is speaking.

ISLAMIC LAW

As Islamic law encompasses a broad range of actions, the scope of legal pronouncements on women is vast, including areas of personal status law, marital and family relations, general legal rights and obligations, questions of property holding, inheritance, criminal law, worship patterns, political rights, and obligations. Women's dress, not generally a legal question, is also included.

Islamic law (*shari'a*) has been described as religious belief applied to the practical problems and affairs of daily living (Fluehr-Lobban 1987). As the problems of daily life change and Muslims adjust to factors new to Muslim society, the Islamic process of law is expected to keep pace and provide answers to these new questions. Building upon Islamic principles, twentieth-century Muslim nations have introduced adaptations into the Islamic legal system to better reflect the needs of their populations.

The reference point for all Islam is the Qur'an, the book of revelations received by the Prophet Muhammad (d. 732 C.E.). The words and actions of the Prophet Muhammad (*Sunna*) supplement the Qur'an. The Sunna has been written and compiled into collections of texts (*hadith*). Muslim scholars have analyzed and historically codified the hadith into authoritative compilations of narratives, traditions, and lists of persons who relayed the accounts. The hadith are accepted as a source of law.

For Muslim scholars of religion (*'ulama*), studying these texts is key to any understanding of how life should be lived. Scholars formulated Qur'anic exegesis and jurisprudence texts in the centuries following the death of Muhammad using Qur'anic passages and hadith texts. Jurists took up questions on women's status by surveying the Qur'an, Sunna, and hadith sources to develop their positions. The practice of the different communities of Muslims was also an influence.

The Qur'an is the supreme source for any questions concerning Islam. Well-regarded hadith texts follow next in importance. The jurisprudence texts utilize these sources of law to work out legal pronouncements. When cases are not immediately clear, jurists may reason by analogy from similar texts in the Qur'an, Sunna, hadith, or writing of distinguished scholars of Islam.

As much of the Qur'an concerns questions of community relations and recommends methods of interpersonal interaction, it discusses aspects of life that affect women. In addition, the Qur'an speaks of female characters—Eve, Hagar, and Mary. These women, along with early female figures of Islam—Khadija,

'Aisha, Fatima, Zainab—are revered as models of Muslim values. Their behavior and words are scrutinized and mythologized to serve as guides for proper Muslim female rectitude.

Unlike Western legal systems, Islamic law conceives of all areas of life as regulated by values revealed in the Qur'an. Within the framework of Islamic *fiqh* (jurisprudence), the actions of Muslims are rated along a scale that ranges from required to prohibited. The five distinctions are *fard* or *wajib* (obligatory); *mandub* (recommended); *ja'iz* (permissible, religiously indifferent); *makruh* (reprehensible, omission preferred, but not punished); and *haram* (forbidden). To give a sense of the broad range of activities regulated by Islamic law, actions that are forbidden range from murder, adultery, theft, and marriage to more than four wives to the eating of pork. Islamic law designates whether practices are permitted or not and, by indicating official community views, seeks to order Muslim society to best achieve community goals.

Four schools of Islamic law (Maliki, Hanafi, Shafi'i, Hanbali) reflect differences in practice in the Sunni community. An example of a major variation is the question of who consents to the marriage. The Maliki school gives the guardian of the bride the right of final consent in marriage. The Hanafi school gives the bride the right to final consent (although consent may be a modest silence). However, the Maliki school grants the wife the right to review the marriage and seek divorce if wished, laying down her grievances before the judge. This right was designed as redress for the right of compulsory marriage that her father or guardian held at the time of her marriage (Borraman 1966, 10). This is still a feature in the Moroccan Personal Status Code.

Judges traditionally respect disparities among the various schools and historically have honored rulings from other schools when applicable. The Shi'a community has its own set of legal precepts, akin to the Sunni schools but with major differences in the area of personal status law such as the practice of temporary (*mut'a*) marriage. Political and doctrinal differences are believed to influence some variations. For example, the greater latitude given to female inheritance among the Shi'a is generally attributed to the prominence of Muhammad's daughter Fatima and her role in guaranteeing succession to the imamate to descendants of her father.

PRE-ISLAMIC ARABIA

Many of the principles of Muslim family law are commonly believed to have been revealed to reform the patriarchal system of pre-Islamic Arabia. In a patriarchal system, authority is vested in the senior male family members and is accepted as a right by other family members. Patriarchy encompasses the subordination of younger males of the unit to older males and the subordination of women to men. Younger women are often considered subordinate to female elders. As the younger women age, they gain authority within their household. While scholars argue whether a matrilineal and matrilocal system existed among a few of the Middle Eastern cultures in pre-Islamic times, all agree that the dominant system was patriarchal and its influence survived the coming of Islam.

Women's status was governed by laws akin to those governing property. Exposing female infants (wa'd) was legal. When of marital age, the wife's male guardian contracted a marriage for her and relinquished rights to her upon payment of the bride-price (mahr). The bride was expected to be a virgin and to be a faithful wife in order to guarantee the paternity of her children. Reflecting the necessity of protecting tribal property, inheritance rights were reserved for mature male relatives. Widows, daughters (who would marry out of their natal family), and minor males were excluded from inheritance. Once married, women were subject to their husband's and his family's control. Men had the right of unlimited polygamy. They also held the right to repudiate a wife and return her to her family. Once repudiated, the wife could be summoned back by her husband at any time to resume marital life. Historical examples, such as the Prophet Muhammad's wives, show us that women exercised independent rights. Khadija had rights to property, hired employees, and ran a successful business. 'Aisha is famed for leading men into battle.

THE QUR'AN ON EQUALITY

Much of the original opposition to Muhammad and his revelation of Islam was due to the egalitarian nature of the new Muslim community. In Islam (submission of oneself to God), the Muslim recognizes God as his or her creator and source of life and blessings. The Qur'an declared a new type of community, no longer ruled by blood-ties and tribal units, but united by allegiance to Islam. The only meaningful distinction, then should be virtue and piety:

> O people! We have created (all of you) out of male and female, and we have made you into different nations and tribes [only] for mutual identification. The noblest of you in the sight of God is the one (who is) the most righteous of you. God knows well and is best informed (Qur'an 49:13).

> For Muslim men and women, for believing men and women, for devout men and women, for true men and women, for men and women who are patient and constant, for men and women who humble themselves, for men and women who give in charity, for men and women who fast (and deny themselves), for men and women who guard their chastity and for men and women who engage much in God's praise, for them has God prepared forgiveness and great reward (Qur'an 33:35).

> All people are equal, as equal as the teeth of a comb. There is no claim of merit of an Arab over a non-Arab, or of a white over a black person, or of a male over a female. Only God-fearing people merit a preference with God (Hadith of Ahmad Ibn Hanbal).

Important statements of equal treatment for men and women are given in verses discussing property (4:32), labor (3:195), reward for righteous living (16:97, 4:124, 40:40), religious obligations (9:71), punishment for theft (5:38) and adultery (24:2), and modesty (24:30–31). Some jurists claim that these verses establish the equality of men and women. However, other verses are believed to establish the opposite sense. Two verses of the Qur'an with much the same meaning are referred to as definitive in outlining the relation of men and women.

The first is found in a passage on divorce. Women are admonished, once divorced, to wait for three months (idda) to determine whether they are pregnant and not to conceal any pregnancy from their husband. "Women have such honorable rights as obligations, but their men have a degree above them" (Qur'an 2:228). An alternate translation renders the verse "And they [women] have rights similar to those (of men) over them in kindness, and men are a degree above women." This is generally taken as meaning that men are superior to women. Another view is that men have a greater responsibility to provide for women.

The other verse reads, "Men are in charge of women, because God has made the one of them to excel the other, and because they spend of their property [for the support of women]" (4:34). This verse refers to the Qur'anic injunction that men must support the women of their household. Some take it as a sign of male superiority; a minority sees it as a material obligation. These two verses have been used as solid reference points for jurists seeking to demonstrate the subordination of women.

Other verses detail situations where women are not to be treated the same as men. These include marriage contracts, repudiation of marriage, inheritance shares, and witnessing. Proponents of various positions on the issue of women's status use different methodologies of reasoning from Qur'anic texts to support their position.

WOMEN'S ECONOMIC STATUS

A major principle of the Qur'an is that of establishing a just society, one concerned with socioeconomic equality among its component parts. The treatment of women and children, as well as reformation of the institution of slavery, were important elements in this concern with establishing an ethical and viable social order. Muhammad criticized Meccan society for its disregard for the welfare of its weaker members; as an orphan, he had personal acquaintance with the treatment meted out to anyone without powerful support.

Many of the reforms of pre-Islamic customs stipulated in the Qur'an concerned the well-being of women and children, particularly girls. Female infanticide (wa'd)—whether for reasons of honor or poverty—was abolished. Reforms were made to ameliorate some injustices committed by men within their families by regulating marriage, bride-price, divorce, and inheritance. The Qur'an underlines the right of women to own and control their own property. Many of the underprivileged referred to in the Qur'an were women. The Qur'an recommends both general and specific action to furnish aid. General injunctions include the right of the indigent to a share of the abundance of the wealthy.

And in their wealth and possessions [was remembered] the right of the [needy], him who asked and he who was prevented [from asking] (Qur'an 51:19, also 70:24–5).

Did you see the one who gives the lie to the Faith? It is he who maltreats orphans and works little for the feeding of the poor. Woe betide then, those who pray, yet are neglectful of their prayers—those who pray for show and even deny the use of their utensils [to the poor] (Qur'an 107:1–7, also 89:15–20).

Specific injunctions recommend express measures to better care for the poor and orphaned. Muhammad himself, following

the death of his first wife, Khadija, set an example for his community by marrying widows and bringing them under his care. Some
Muslims consider the scripture that allows the men to marry up
to four women to be an injunction to care for the orphaned and
less fortunate. If one reads it in context, the passage takes on a
different meaning than simple permission to marry four wives if
they can be treated equally.

> Give the orphans their property and do not exchange the corrupt for
> the good; and devour not their property with your property; sure
> that is a great crime. If you fear that you will not act justly towards
> the orphans, marry such women as seem good to you, two, three,
> four; but if you fear you will not be equitable, then only one, or
> what your right hands own; so it is likelier you will not be partial
> (Qur'an 4: 2–3).

If one has doubts about caring for orphans, or not cheating
them of their property, then the men should marry a few orphans—but be sure to treat all wives equitably. This question of
equitable treatment of wives is emphasized; some contemporary
Muslims see it as an implicit prohibition of polygamy, as no man
can treat two wives—much less four—equally.

Women, seen as more vulnerable, are always to be represented
by or under the care of a male relative to absorb any unwanted
dealings with the world outside their home. Nonetheless, women
own and manage their own property absolutely and have no obligation to contribute their resources to the family. Given the male
responsibility to care for the women within his purview and the
firm Muslim convictions on the unalienable nature of property,
inheritance becomes a difficult question. The Qur'an solves it by
giving women a share but making it less than that of the men,
who are obliged by family ties to care for female relatives.

EDUCATION

In education, practices of a given culture or tradition may differ from Qur'anic precepts. While Islam firmly maintains the value of education for all, many Muslim countries have not worked to extend educational opportunities and facilities to women to the same extent as to men. These educational policies doubtless reflect cultural mores that restrict the entrance of women into public life. The result is imbalance in the educational status of men and women in the majority of Muslim countries. The literacy rate of women is often one-third that of men.

Hadith texts emphasize the importance of education to the Muslim community, to men, and to women. A popular hadith states, "Seek education, even if it be in China." Another hadith emphasizes the role of the father in educating his daughters: "The father, if he educates his daughter well, will enter paradise." Another popular saying attributed to al-Shawki states, "A mother is a school. If she is educated, than a whole people are educated."

The majority of Muslim states have pulled their educational policies in line with religious precepts by making education available to girls as well as boys. Constraints still exist in the amount of resources available to devote to education, but strides have been made in most countries. In some cases, like that of Saudi Arabia, governments resist coeducational education and prefer to educate boys and girls and men and women in separate facilities.

Education holds a vital place in how Islam itself is perceived. Research done on family planning in the Middle East demonstrates that educational levels of religious leaders play a role in the position they take on contraceptive use. More educated 'ulama tend to be far more open to family-planning measures than poorly educated, local-level religious leaders (Bowen 1980).

Islamic Law and the Status of Women

Islamic law comprises different subcategories of law including, among others, family law, property law, criminal law, and contract law. While some areas of law have a great deal to say about women's status and behavior, others differentiate little between men and women.

Islam imposed dramatic reforms upon Arabs used to the pre-Islamic customs whereby women fell under the domination of their male relatives or husbands in the household. The Qur'anic reforms were substantial, and Muslim women held considerable rights compared to women of most cultures, Western and Eastern, until the feminist movements of the twentieth century forced reforms.

Although the Qur'anic reforms fundamentally bettered the position of women, shari'a outlined a social system where women defer to men and where men are assigned responsibility for the care of women in their household. The subservience, however, lies within a larger context of Qur'anic reforms—the transference of the focus of concern from the tribe to the community and, within the community, to smaller family units.

The society postulated in the Qur'an achieves a balance and coherence that was considered to suit the needs of its community. The designed balance, however, depends upon the good working of each part of society. If any piece falls out of line, the whole social mechanism is endangered, as it depends upon the meshing of each part with the others. The intermeshing of the pieces of the family law—working to achieve the goals of the society without weighing the needs of individuals—could be seen as equitable. If pieces of family law are isolated and examined as to equality or equity, then the disparity between men's and women's rights is clear. In other words, the system operates as a whole within the Qur'anic guidelines, but the introduction of one glitch can scuttle the intent of the family-law system. A good example is inheritance. A woman generally inherits half of what a man (in the same relation to the deceased) inherits. The reasoning follows that a woman can rely upon her male family members to support her. She, therefore, has less need of the inheritance than a man who is responsible for the support of women in his family. If male relatives fail to supply this support or deny her access to her inheritance, the intent of the law is scuttled, and the woman is disadvantaged despite a theoretically coherent system.

Part of the difficulty in analyzing Muslim family law lies in the intersection of sectors being analyzed given the size of the Muslim world and the diversity of the societies that adhere to Islam. Despite the reforms of Islam, the patriarchal system inherited from the pre-Islamic Arabs still exercises enormous influence that can be seen in the impact of customary practices upon Islamic law. In addition, many traditions have been built up around the law. Finally, the coherence of shari'a, like any legal system, lies in the good faith of its citizens. The Qur'an calls for Muslims to act in kindness and generosity and to guard the best interests of others. Unfortunately, no legal system has been able to guarantee the rectitude of its citizens.

The basic precepts of Islamic family law are described in broad strokes in what follows; reforms made in the last century are treated in a separate section. Shari'a regards the woman as a perpetual minor. She remains for her lifetime under the guardianship of a male relative (e.g., father, uncle, brother, son) or court-appointed guardian (*wali*). The guardian retains the right to contract marriage for the woman and to arrange her bride-price of which she is entitled to one-half. The woman's consent is not needed for the marriage. In the Maliki school, that of the guardian is sufficient; in the Hanafi school, silence is taken as consent.

Although the husband has exclusive right to the woman's sexual attentions and may return her to her home if she is not virgin, the husband may contract up to three other marriages, and historically, could maintain relations with concubines (his female slaves), whose children would be recognized as his heirs.

Prosecuting men for adultery is difficult since the wife has no claim upon the body of her husband.

Divorce is properly termed repudiation and is not reciprocal. The husband has the right to repudiate the wife without giving a reason. The wife has only limited rights to initiate divorce and depends on a judge to grant her divorce. In case of divorce, custody of the children passes from the mother to the father when the boy or girl is seven or nine respectively. In inheritance, the woman generally receives half the share given the man who stands in the same relation to the deceased.

If one reads the Qur'an carefully, it is evident that it ordains a new society, one, nonetheless, firmly rooted in the conventions of pre-Islamic Arabia. While the Islamic community (*umma*), with its emphasis on equality of the believers and guarantees of social and economic justice, provides the framework for the new society, the basic unit remains the family. Within this family structure, each gender has a role. Men—physically more powerful—are given the duty of providing wherewithal for the family. As women bear and nurse children, they order domestic life and care for the children. As the emphasis is upon the family, no individual is conceived of as being alone or apart from the group.

The intent of the Qur'an seems to be less to work out equal justice for each believer than to construct a coherent system that will care for all its adherents, seeing that the poor as well as the affluent are well cared for in the Muslim community. Gender considerations are secondary to community order.

PERSONAL STATUS LAW

Family or personal status law governs male and female interactions in the family and has more to say concerning women than other areas of law. This body of law demonstrates the dominant position of men in Islamic society by their greater number of legal rights. Family law also notes men's obligations to provide for the needs of the women. The Qur'anic statement that "men have a degree above women" (2:228) is here illustrated in that men have greater privileges than women but, likewise, have greater responsibilities for their care.

In family law, the four schools of Sunni law and the Shi'i schools of law vary in different areas. To simplify matters, this chapter does not record the diversity of adaptations and modifications made by each school. If the practice is widely followed, it is presented as general practice. In exceptions to general practice, the school's variation is noted.

MARRIAGE

Marriage (nikah) is recognized as essential to an orderly society and described as a legal commitment sanctioned by God and acknowledged by society (Abdul-Rauf 1977, 39). It is a civil contract permitting intercourse and the procreation of children. As a contract, it necessitates an offer by one party and an acceptance by the other. The woman is expected to be represented by her guardian (wali), who may be her father or a close male relative; lacking any family member, the judge himself may serve as her guardian. The woman has the right to accept or reject the marriage arranged by her guardian. Silence on her part is construed as consent. In the Hanafi school, if the bride is a minor, she will have the right to repudiate the marriage upon reaching her majority (khiyar al-bulugh). The Maliki school grants the right of a khlu' divorce to minor brides upon her reevaluation. Boys who marry before their majority have the same right to repudiate the marriage upon coming of age.

A man may marry a Jewish, Christian, or Zoroastrian woman (kitabiyya) from among the religious communities who have written scriptures and enjoy an elevated status among Muslims. A Muslim woman may only marry a Muslim man.

Men and women are enjoined from marrying family members in certain blood relationships (e.g., ascendants, lineal descendants, offspring of grandparents; however, marriage with children of maternal and paternal uncles is permitted). They are also forbidden to marry various relatives of their spouse (e.g., wife's mother and grandmother; for details see Abu Zahra 1955, 3). The milk tie, a legal relationship between the infant suckled and the woman giving suck and her husband, precludes marriage with any of the milk mother's children or certain categories of her relatives. The prohibitions parallel that of marrying relatives (Abu Zahra 1955, 4). In recent years, a Jordanian woman, determined to extricate herself from her marriage, suckled the breast of her mother-in-law in order to establish a milk relationship and forbid further sexual relations between herself and her husband, now her milk-brother (Antoun 1990, 51–3).

Men are also forbidden to contract marriages with the wives of other men or with a woman who is in 'idda, a period of time that determines whether the woman is pregnant and verifies paternity of the child. When the 'idda has passed (three months for a divorced woman, four months and ten days for a widow), the couple is free to marry.

EQUALITY OF STATUS

The Hanafi school holds a secondary doctrine concerning marriage, the rule of equality, which states that the husband should be an equal in social status to the woman. Marriage raises a woman to her husband's status (Esposito 1982a, 22). The Maliki school disagrees and holds that equality in religion, that is, both being good Muslims, is the only criterion in determining marriageability (Fluehr-Lobban 1987, 89).

POLYGYNY

A Muslim husband is permitted to have up to four wives. The condition understood from the Qur'anic permission is that the wives must be treated equitably. Muslim women are permitted one husband. Marriage to a second husband is considered void.

TEMPORARY MARRIAGE (MUT'A)

Shi'i Muslims recognize a marriage set for a fixed term (usually entailing a prearranged financial agreement), affirmed in a contract by both the man and the woman. Sunni Muslims prohibit this practice, considering it to be little short of prostitution (Momen 1985, 182). Mut'a marriages are a system for regularizing sexual contact when the husband finds himself away from home for protracted periods, such as on a pilgrimage.

BRIDE-PRICE (MAHR)

The bride-price (mahr) is intended to secure the wife's economic status after marriage and is an indispensable part of every marriage contract (Qur'an 4:4). Islamic law requires the husband to pay the bride-price to the wife, not to the wife's father. Traditionally, the wife's guardian controlled the bride-price just as he took responsibility for all the family's economic obligations. Commonly, half the bride-price is held in abeyance, payable in case of divorce, although a far more than half may be held. This gives the husband a financial interest in remaining married. Extensive legal controls are stipulated that guard the payment of the bride-price (the unpaid portion) for the wife or her heirs. If the union is dissolved prior to consummation, half the bride-price belongs to the bride (Qur'an 2:236, 2:237).

DUTIES OF THE WIFE

The wife's obligations to her husband and her family are simply stated: She maintains the home, bears and cares for her children, and obeys her husband.

DUTIES OF THE HUSBAND

The husband's major duty is maintenance (food, clothing, lodging) for his wife first and secondarily for his children. He owes his wife maintenance (no matter what her personal resources)

as she owes him fidelity and obedience. If his cruelty or nonpay-
ment of bride-price occasion her disobedience, he still owes her
maintenance. Maintenance is also owed to an unmarried daughter,
whatever her age, and a widowed or divorced daughter if she is
ill (Esposito 1982a, 27). Jurisprudence texts agree that the wife
has the right to sexual fulfillment and the right to have children
(Bowen 1981).

REPUDIATION

Divorce is more properly termed repudiation (*talaq*), as the right
to dissolve the marriage rests with the husband. The laws governing divorce are complicated and center upon proper and kind
treatment of the wife. Divorce, while permitted, is disapproved
of in all Qur'anic pronouncements. To lessen its negative impact,
considerate patterns of divorce are recommended. In all forms,
the husband pronounces intent to divorce. At this point, the wife
often returns to her family and waits a period of time ('idda) to
determine if she is pregnant. If not pregnant, the 'idda continues
for three menstrual cycles; if she is pregnant, it continues until
she bears the child.

The pronouncement of divorce can be revoked, and the wife
may resume marital life with her husband at any time during the
'idda. In most schools, the husband may repudiate and reclaim
his wife two times. At the declaration of the third repudiation,
the marriage is dissolved. Remarriage between the former spouses
is prohibited unless the wife marries another, consummates the
marriage, and then is widowed or divorced. A disapproved type
of repudiation is *talaq al-bidah*, which resembles the capricious,
one-sided divorce prevalent in pre-Islamic times. Here the husband pronounces the divorce three times in succession or says "I
divorce you three times," and the marriage ends.

Variations that grant more discretion over the divorce to
the wife include delegated divorce (*talaq al-tafwid*), whereby the
husband grants the wife the power to divorce when he offers her

the option by using words such as "choose" or "divorce yourself" (Esposito 1982a, 33). In khul' or *mubaraah* divorce, the divorce is mutually agreed upon. In khul' divorces, the wife offers to give up some or all of her bride-price to her husband. In mubaraah divorce, both mutually want a separation (Esposito 1982a, 34). This is an irrevocable divorce.

Two court-determined divorces, *lian* and *faskh*, can be pronounced by the judge. Lian divorces concern oaths made by the partners in accusation of adultery. If the problem is unresolved by the spouses, the judge may dissolve the marriage. Faskh divorces grant the judge the power to dissolve a marriage at the request of the wife. The schools of law disagree as to proper grounds. The Hanafi school presents the narrowest grounds and allows the court to dissolve a marriage in defined conditions: the marriage was not properly undertaken, a husband is unable to consummate the marriage, or the husband is missing, in which case the wife is declared a putative widow. As Hanafi law was the most restrictive in granting divorce to women, Hanafi jurists clearly conceded that, if application of their reading of divorce law caused hardship to a woman, judges were permitted to apply appropriate Maliki, Shafi'i, or Hanbali provisions (Fyzee 1974, 169).

Maliki law is the most generous in granting divorces upon a woman's petition. Grounds are cruelty, refusal or inability to maintain the wife, desertion, and serious disease or ailment that would make continuing the marriage harmful to the wife. If the divorce were granted, the bride-price would be returned to the husband. The Shafi'i and Hanbali schools fall between the Hanbali and Maliki schools' positions on divorce for women (Esposito 1982a, 36). If the husband or the wife renounces Islam (apostasy), the marriage is considered void.

Shi'i law makes divorce more difficult. Shi'a allow only the preferred divorce (*talaq al-sunna*) and not the innovative divorce (*talaq al-bidah*), wherein the husband may incur a final divorce by stating three times that he divorces his wife. Shi'a require that the statement of divorce be made in front of two witnesses and do not allow a statement of divorce if the husband is intoxicated or furious (Momen 1985, 183).

Since divorce dissolves the marriage that is bound by a contract, women may stipulate in their marriage contract that they have the right to divorce in certain circumstances, such as the taking of a second wife. This is the case in Iran and Morocco, among other countries.

CUSTODY

In the case of a divorce, custody of children is determined by the age of the child. During the early years of childhood (*hidana*, or age of dependence), the child remains with the mother or the mother's family. At the age of seven for a male child and nine for a female child (for some jurists, nine for a male child and eleven for a female child), the father or father's family receives custody of the child (Abu Zahra 1955, 22). Schools differ at what age the children leave to go to their father's home.

During the period of the mother's custody, the father or nearest male agnate relative remains the guardian of the child. He has the right to control the child's education and to contract a marriage for the child (without the mother's permission). The mother may lose custody if she is judged morally or physically unfit to care for the child (Coulson and Hinchcliffe 1978, 45).

INHERITANCE

Islamic laws of inheritance, renowned for their complexity, are closely tied to social expectations of families and gender roles. The reform in inheritance law reflected the shift in emphasis from the tribe and validated the greater responsibility of care for the family vested in the male family members. Under Qur'anic reforms in inheritance, women heirs generally receive a share one-half that of the male heirs, as men are responsible for care of the women.

Heirs cannot be instituted under Islamic law. The testator can act at his or her discretion only in making legacies and in naming an executor. Beyond that, the Islamic law of inheritance applies, and shares of inheritance are set and distributed among family members. Four other classes of heirs, legally determined and of no relation to the deceased, may in rare cases inherit (Esposito 1982b, 44).

Inheritance falls to three major classes of heirs; the first category is heirs stipulated in the Qur'an (ashab al-furud), who are guaranteed an assured share of the inheritance. The second is agnates; the third category, failing heirs in the first categories, is cognates. The first category of heirs includes the husband or wife, the father, the mother, sons, daughters, paternal grandfather, maternal grandmother, son's daughter, full sister, consanguine sister, and uterine brother and uterine sister. Many of these can be excluded by the presence of assured heirs who rank higher in the hierarchy (e.g., the maternal grandmother is excluded if the mother of the deceased is living; the full sister can be excluded by the existence of a son, father, or paternal grandfather.) The share of each can be increased or decreased according to the existence of other heirs. Although this category of heirs inherits first, they only receive a portion of the estate.

Male and female rights differ in inheritance. The wife inherits one-fourth of the husband's estate if there are no children and one-eighth if there are children. The husband inherits one-half of the wife's estate is there are no children and one-fourth if there are children. The rationale for women inheriting less than men centers on the responsibility of male relatives to provide for womenfolk: fathers for daughters, brothers for sisters, sons for mothers, male guardians for unmarried women. Within this large extended family safety net, individuals are buffered from want or need. Studies on inheritance have demonstrated that the strict rules of inheritance are influenced by circumstances. As male labor is necessary for working land, many women choose not to inherit land but to take their inheritance in jewelry or even a room in the parental house to be used in case of divorce. Other women, having inherited a piece of land, leave it to male relatives to work and take a percentage of profits (Gerhom 1985).

In Shi'i law, to the contrary of Sunni law, when males and females are of equal close relation to the deceased, the females are not excluded to the benefit of the male (as in the inheritance of the agnatic relatives), although the share of the male is still twice that of the female (Momen 1955, 183). In particular, this applies to the advantage of daughters (with no brothers) at the death of their father. Here the rights of the daughter allow her to inherit a full share to the exclusion of male agnates.

In practice, in many parts of the Muslim world, custom over-whelms Qur'anic prescriptions, resulting in inheritance patterns far from the Qur'anic norm. In general, this works to the dis-advantage of female heirs. The most common customary practice is to deny female heirs their inheritance (Levy 1965, 244–5).

Islamic law allows for legacies to be made for up to one-third of an estate. Also, property holders have the option of making gifts of their property before their death. Estates were passed whole to a son or male relative to limit fragmentation. Husbands who felt their wives or daughters would inherit too little could leave them properties as a legacy (Schacht 1990).

Another Islamic institution, the *waqf,* may be utilized as a means of guaranteeing an inheritance. By designating an endow-ment of property for the benefit of particular heirs, or by putting the administration of a waqf in the hands of specific relatives, the property remained an endowment in perpetuity guaranteeing income to that person or persons and their heirs. As *awqaf* (plural of waqf) can circumvent inheritance laws, they could be used to benefit a daughter or other female relative and guarantee her a chosen amount, equal to that of males if desired.

At periods in Islamic history, women, particularly those of elite status (for whom we have better records), were entrusted with family property. Various reasons facilitated women's control over property. In general, women were valued for their ability to guarantee family stability and continuity of the lineage. In actuarial terms, they were a better risk than men as they married young and were insulated by their gender from the warfare and feuding that occupied men. As women held the right to litigate to defend their rights and property, they were at no disadvantage in preserving the interests of the family (Petry 1991).

Other Areas of Law

PROPERTY

Islam holds that, since the ownership of everything belongs to God, all individuals have a share in its resources. As the law of inheritance permits women to own property, women are encouraged to participate in economic activities (Mannan 1986, 359–61). Under Islamic law, property is held absolutely by free men and free women. Although spouses may inherit from each other, neither acquires an interest in the other's property through marriage. The wife is entitled to maintenance from the husband during his life; at his death, she only inherits the percentage of property stipulated (one-fourth or one-eighth of the estate) in Qur'anic inheritance laws. Legally, men have no claim on property owned by their wives.

PROCEDURE

The major issue concerning gender in procedural law is the question of witnesses. In a lawsuit, two men or one man and two women may testify as witnesses. In addition, the evidence of two women may only be accepted as valid concerning matters in which women have special expertise (e.g., birth, virginity, etc.) (Schacht 1964, 193). A woman may qualify to be a judge (*qadi*), but may not preside in cases involving criminal (*hadd*) punishments (see section on criminal law) (Schacht 1964, 198).

CRIMINAL LAW OR PENAL LAW

Islamic shari'a has no categories equivalent to the Western concept of criminal law. Since the nineteenth- and twentieth-century reforms of legal codes, categories of criminal law have emerged. These criminal codes are based on Western, rather than Islamic, law. Three categories of Islamic shari'a demand punishment: hadd or *huddud* punishments, *jinayat*, and special cases affecting community decorum.

The Qur'an specifies crimes punishable by hadd, including unlawful intercourse *(zina)*, false accusation of unlawful intercourse, impugning the legitimacy of a child (an accusation directed against women), drinking wine, theft, and highway robbery. Hadd punishments range from stoning to death (most severe punishment for unlawful intercourse), to flogging, to cutting off the hand or foot (theft). The severity of the punishment depends on the circumstances of the crime, the discretion of the judge, any repentance on the part of the accused, and the status of the accused. Slaves are allotted half the lashes dealt out to a free person. In addition, slaves, even if convicted of unlawful intercourse, may not be stoned to death. For the hadd punishment to be levied, the testimony of four male witnesses, all of whom must be free men, is required for the accusation to be valid (Schacht 1964, 174–9).

Jinayat deals with private vengeance. This category derives from pre-Islamic custom (although sanctioned in Islamic law) and is treated akin to crimes against property.

The third area concerns special cases that may be undertaken to maintain public decorum and uphold community values. An example that involves gender issues is apostasy from Islam. The male apostate is executed, although shari'a recommends giving him three days to recant his conversion. A female apostate is imprisoned and beaten every three days until she returns to Islam (Schacht 1964, 187).

While no allowances are made for gender in the general discussion of the law, present-day discussions of different treatment for similar offenses suggest a double standard. This works at times for, at times against, women's interest.

CONTRACTS AND OBLIGATIONS

No differences are drawn between men and women in their ability to negotiate, contract, or litigate contracts and agreements. Both may litigate in defense of their property rights (Schacht 1964, 144–50). No qualifications are placed on the sale, lease, ratification, or cancellation of contracts by gender. Women are not excluded from formation of partnerships, corporations, or other business ventures by law. Nor are they excepted from liability in case of damages or torts.

CONSTITUTIONAL LAW OR GOVERNMENT

Nowhere in the Qur'an are women granted the right to rule their community; neither are they expressly prohibited. The most influential reference is a widely quoted hadith of the Prophet: "The people who make a woman their ruler are past saving." Few women have ruled sections of the Islamic empire (e.g., Shajar al-Durr of Mamluk Egypt, d. 1257).

WORSHIP

The obligations of Muslims towards ritual worship are contained in the five pillars of Islam: adherence to the creed (shahada), prayer (salat), tithes (zakat), fasting during Ramadan, and the pilgrimage to Mecca (hajj). Islamic law also categorizes actions by permissibility ranging from what is incumbent upon the faithful Muslim to what is prohibited to him or her. None of these obligations are affected by gender, and all obligations apply equally to male and female adults, although expectations as to their practice may differ somewhat. Religious precepts and rules of worship are based on the concept of all Muslims being equal before God.

All Muslims are expected to follow principles laid down in the law. However, women are expected to follow different conduct in religious practice.

Differences in practice are recommended for separate obligations. For example, women are expected to pray at home or, when in the mosque, to pray out of sight behind the assembled men. Women who make the pilgrimage to Mecca wear a different garment. Women are restricted from performing religious obligations when considered impure, which is while menstruating or following the birth of a child. At this time, women are not permitted to fast or pray formally, but they are expected to fast an equivalent period to compensate for those days at another time of the year. Both women and men are required to follow the axioms of religious worship.

TWENTIETH-CENTURY LEGAL REFORMS IN SHARI'A

Demands for reform in family law have been voiced in various countries, led by Egypt and India, responding to a growing national consensus for change. A major impetus for reform has been the example of Western codes of family law. As Islamic law is based upon the Qur'an—revelations from God, many Muslims resist any suggestions of change. Many reformers use a Qur'anic verse to suggest the possibility of adapting to changing circumstances: "Verily, God changes not what a people has until they change it for themselves" (Qur'an 13:12). (An alternate translation reads, "Lo, Allah changes not the condition of a folk until they [first] change that which is in their hearts." M. M. Pickthall translation.)

The justification for reforms has generally been argued by citing the intent of the Qur'an. However, a tension exists among different groups of Muslims as to whether Islamic law can be reformed. Many of the legal reforms discussed below are neither inspired by the Qur'an nor necessarily rooted in Islamic law.

Many reforms are influenced more by European than Muslim practices.

An example would be the legal age for marriage, an area upon which the Qur'an is silent. Many reforms are attempted within the context or connotations of Islamic law, so that reformers in some areas attempt to expand the possible interpretations of Islamic law or to use Islamically sanctioned methods (recourse to judicial decree or arbitration) to achieve similar results. Many Middle Eastern nations in promulgating reforms have preserved core Islamic legal principles, such as the unchallenged right of the man to repudiate his wife, while stressing other ethical principles integral to Islam, such as the right of redress of wrongs, right of maintenance, right of considerate treatment, and right to mediation to resolve problems. This allows greater latitude for women seeking divorce from untenable marriages.

Turkey effected the most dramatic reform of personal status law when it abandoned religious law in the 1920s and replaced it with the Swiss Civil Code. The reforms of other Muslim states have not been comprehensive. Many kept personal status legislation within the scope of shari'a. With few exceptions (e.g., Saudi Arabia), most legal codes derived from or modeled on Islamic law have been reviewed over the course of this century to grant women greater rights. The rise of Islamic activist movements and their emphasis upon strict interpretations of women's conduct has resulted in the limitation or revoking of reforms. Following the 1979 revolution in Iran, the new government revoked reforms legislated during the Shah's era.

Other countries have modified their reforms. In Egypt, legal remedies to grant women greater rights have proved a constant political battleground. Reforms such as restrictions on the husband's right to polygamy have been promulgated, revoked, and then restored. We must assume that the trend toward democracy, when coupled with strong activist or Islamist sentiment, will jeopardize many women's status reforms. On the positive side, both Egypt and Morocco have introduced reforms and are pressured continually to extend the reforms further.

While most Muslim states used shari'a as a basis for personal status law, they patterned other areas of their legal codes on Western models. In many cases, their constitutions and legal codes are based on Western codes. Even Pakistan, which proclaims itself a Muslim state, bases part of its legal system, the commercial code, on English common law.

MARRIAGE

Reforms that raise the age of marriage have proved simple to legislate but difficult to enforce. A concomitant area is that of marriage registration. In 1923, Egypt legislated that the age of marriage for women be sixteen and for men eighteen (Esposito 1982a, 52). Subsequent rulings by other Muslim states have raised the age of marriage for women to seventeen or eighteen. However, because of a lack of documentation (birth certificates, identity cards, etc.) attesting to their age, marriage requirements for women are difficult to implement (White 1978, 55). Authorities had little recourse in administering the law beyond refusing to register marriages of underage women. Another drawback is that rigorous enforcement of this statute on the local level is impossible without the support of local government officials, notably the village and city-quarter officials who know the families and marriageable daughters well enough to seize upon violations of the law.

The difficult question of polygamy is a major area for marriage reform. Many reformers opposed polygamy and argued that, according to the shari'a, monogamy was the choice of Islam. They took as their source the qualification of equitable treatment ("but if you fear you will not be equitable, then [marry] only one" Qur'an 4:3). Since it is impossible to treat one wife exactly as another, they stated, the verse urges monogamy.

Only a few countries outlaw polygamy. Among them, Turkey

and Tunisia are the only Middle Eastern states with a majority of Muslim citizens. The others are Israel, states comprising republics of the former Soviet Union, and the Isma'ilis of East Africa (e.g., Kenya and Tanzania). Reforms, however, have been introduced to limit the extent of polygamy. Measures have been legislated to give the wife a voice in this decision. Generally, the husband was required to request permission from a state agency before contracting a plural marriage.

In prerevolutionary Iran, the husband had to petition the court (Coulson and Hinchcliffe 1978, 40). In Pakistan, the husband must obtain permission from an Arbitration Council, whose membership includes the head of the local union council and representatives of both the husband and the wife (Coulson and Hinchcliffe 1978, 40; Esposito 1982a, 84). It is the council's job to determine whether the plural marriage is "necessary and just." Without the agreement of the wife, consent is difficult to obtain. Husbands who marry in contravention of these statutory provisions contract valid marriages, but the husband is liable to criminal prosecution, and the first wife may receive dissolution of the marriage and demand the full bride-price due her (in the case of Pakistan). Circumstances that may lead a judge or a council to rule for polygamous marriages include the insanity of the wife; her contracting an incurable disease; her addiction to drugs, alcohol, or gambling; her imprisonment for five or more years; her abandonment of the family; or her sterility (Coulson and Hinchcliffe 1978, 40).

Most Muslim states allow a bride to add a clause to the marriage contract declaring that her husband will not seek a second wife without her permission (Coulson and Hinchcliffe 1978, 40; Royaume de Maroc 1957, art. 31). If this stipulation is violated, she has the right to dissolution of the marriage. The Moroccan law is not explicit on whether the first or second marriage will be dissolved; the matter lies in the hands of the judge who holds the wife's petition for a hearing.

In Egypt, the personal status amendments of 1979 required a man to officially notify his wife if he took a second wife. If she objected, she could divorce him, receive alimony, and retain custody of young children. A controversial stipulation of the amendments in housing-poor Egypt held that the woman had the right to the family apartment or another that the husband was to provide. Islamic activists vocally objected to the law and attempted to have it struck down. In 1985, the constitutionality of the law was challenged. As Anwar Sadat had used presidential privilege to pass the law by decree, the courts could not support this use of emergency law measures. The result was that the law was repealed. This left Egypt under the 1920 and 1929 rulings that the husband does not need to officially inform his wife if he takes a second wife, nor is a second marriage automatic grounds for divorce or custody of the children (Hijab1988, 29–31). Many of the reforms have since been reinstated but not the controversial section that granted the woman rights to divorce and the apartment. In January 2000, the Egyptian Law of Personal Status was amended giving women greater access to divorce.

In 1992, Moroccan women's rights activists initiated a one-million-signature campaign to reform the personal status code. After much discussion and opposition, reforms were codified in the personal status code in 1993. These reforms included requiring the consent and signature of the intended wife to the marriage contract; allowing women over the age of eighteen whose fathers are deceased to contract their marriage without a guardian's permission; allowing a woman to include a clause in the marriage contract reserving the right to ask for a divorce if her husband marries additional wives; and granting women whose husbands are deceased or incapacitated the legal custody of their children. In 2001, women petitioned for additional reforms that include raising the minimum age of marriage for girls and women from fifteen to eighteen; outlawing polygamy except in certain cases; giving women after a divorce the right to half of the property acquired during the marriage; and allowing divorced mothers to retain custody of their children if they remarry.

Yemen has worked to establish rights for women. However, the Constitution of unified Yemen retreats from specific reforms established in the 1974 code of personal status of the People's Democratic Republic of Yemen. The Constitution of Yemen written following the country's 1990 unification guarantees equal rights and duties to both men and women, without distinguishing between them. Rights to political participation, employment, and education are intended to establish women's equality and eliminate discrimination. Special provision to protect women in pregnancy and maternity were also established. The 1992 Law of Personal Status establishes the women's age of marriage at fifteen and protects the right to polygyny. It notes that unless expressly stated in law, shari'a is to serve as the residual source of personal status law. Hadd penalties could also be applied to crimes.

DIVORCE

Islamic law permits divorce but judges divorce reprehensible (makruh)—an act better not committed. Although Qur'anic verses spell out the proper conduct in a divorce, they restrict the license to divorce and to recall wives at will enjoyed by husbands in pre-Islamic times. A well-known hadith establishes that "Divorce is the most hateful thing which God permits." As divorce, or more properly, repudiation (talaq) in Islamic law lies solely in the hands of the husband, reforms in divorce law have centered around giving the wife recourse to request divorce.

In most parts of the Muslim world, legal reforms in the area of divorce have sought to conserve the Islamic system of repudiation while, at the same time, attempting to grant women the right to leave intolerable marriages. The Ottoman Empire in 1915 established desertion or a husband's contagious disease as bases for divorce. Since then other provisions have been added that include failure to provide maintenance, maltreatment, lengthy imprisonment of the husband, husband's insanity, cruel treatment, impotency, and incompatibility of temperament.

In Tunisia and Algeria, more far-reaching reforms allow women to request divorce with no grounds, as long as they are willing to pay financial compensation to their husbands (Coulson and Hinchcliffe 1978, 41–2). In the Sudan, the wife has the right to apply for divorce in a shari'a court, although the husband holds total rights to sue for divorce without establishing grounds. The cultural difficulties inherent in airing one's marital complaints publicly in court has led to the establishment of marriage arbitration conducted by two court-appointed arbitrators, one to represent each spouse (Fluehr-Lobban 1987, 90–1).

The most critical area facing divorce law reformers is the husband's power to repudiate or divorce his wife at will without showing cause. Although unjust divorces are greatly disapproved of in Islam, they are nonetheless valid. The irrevocable talaq al-bid'a, or repudiation of innovation—the type disapproved of in classical jurisprudence—came under scrutiny by the reformers since it can be effected while the husband is drunk or enraged. Since it has the effect of three divorces, the wife is summarily dismissed and the marriage dissolved. (The partners can only remarry if the wife remarries in the interim.) Most countries have enacted reforms to curtail the talaq al-bid'a. Pakistan's legislation has the intent of preventing the divorce from going into effect until arbitration has taken place. Syria, in 1953, legislated mandatory maintenance for a year for women divorced without cause.

Although reforms granted the wife greater access to divorce, the thrust of the divorce laws of most countries leaves ultimate power to dissolve the marriage (and the option of abuse of that power) in the hands of the husband, staying within the intent of the shari'a. Tunisia, South Yemen, and prerevolutionary Iran promulgated laws that gave both spouses equal rights to divorce if the court was convinced that their marital conflicts were irreconcilable. When the two Yemens united, divorce law followed the more conservative Yemen Arab Republic, and women lost equal right to divorce. While Tunisia gave the wife equal rights to divorce, Iran (in the 1975 Iranian Family Protection Law) removed the right of unilateral divorce from the husband.

CHILD CUSTODY

The guiding principle underlying reform of child custody laws has become the welfare of the child, not the right of the father to custody of children. Various legal approaches have been used to achieve this reform. The first Egyptian reforms in 1929 extended the mother's custody until nine years of age for sons and eleven years of age for daughters. In doing so, they utilized a minority opinion of Hanafi law that holds that the custody passes to the father when boys no longer need the services of their mother and girls have reached the age of desire. The majority holds these ages to be seven and nine respectively. In 1979, the law was amended to allow the courts to grant the mother custody if it were deemed in the child's best interests (Esposito 1982a, 56)

In India and Pakistan, judicial decisions have been utilized to extend custody as best befits the needs of the children. In Syria, Tunisia, Iraq, prerevolutionary Iran, and the former South Yemen, legislation decreed that custody may be given to either parent as the court decides will best benefit the children. (Coulson and Hinchcliffe 1978, 45). In Iran, if the father is judged morally unsuitable or a danger to the children, then the court can award the children to the mother or designate another guardian. In reforming custody law, the Sudan has reformed the shari'a by following the most liberal interpretation of classical shari'a. In 1932, Circular Number 34 authorized courts to extend a woman's custody of her children if it is in the interest of the child. This follows the Maliki opinion that permits a woman to retain custody of her son until the age of puberty and of her daughter until the consummation of her marriage. The burden of proof, however, is on the mother. Custody will revert to the former husband at nine years for a girl and seven years for a boy, unless the mother makes an application in court to retain custody. The court then begins an inquiry centering on the best interests of the children. It should be noted that the remarriage of the mother generally works against her chances of retaining custody of the child. Mothers who work outside the home are also regarded unfavorably (Fluehr-Lobban 1993; Coulson and Hinchcliffe 1978, 45).

INHERITANCE

In some countries, custom, rather than Islamic law, has excluded women from inheritance. Enforcement of the Islamic law of inheritance would, in those cases, increase women's property rights. Beyond that, however, reforms of inheritance law are directed at dividing property with increased equality. In Pakistan, Egypt, and other countries, changes in the law have ensured the right of orphaned grandchildren to inherit (Esposito 1982a, 88; White 1978, 57). Other reforms have increased the ability of daughters to inherit. Tunisian reforms stipulate that daughters may exclude male agnatic relatives from inheritance. As the Qur'an states that the presence of a child (*walad*) excludes a brother from inheritance, this reform is in accordance with Sunni law if the word *walad* is understood as child, not male child as traditionally interpreted (Coulson and Hinchcliffe 1978, 47).

Reforms made in the Sudan, Egypt, and Iraq allow males to make bequests to wives or daughters giving them more than the stipulated maximum one-third inheritance. Other nations have further reformed Sunni inheritance law. Somalia has decreed that men and women have equal rights to inheritance. Iraq, in 1963, passed legislation establishing Shi'i inheritance law as the standard for the country, the upshot being that any child, whether male or female, excludes collateral relatives and more remote relatives from inheritance (Coulson and Hinchcliffe 1978, 47).

CRIMINAL LAW

Criminal law is not a subcategory of personal status law. It is included in this chapter because reforms in the understanding of criminal law have had a significant effect upon women. The criminal code referred to in this chapter is that of Egypt. Egypt, like many other Muslim countries (notable exceptions are Pakistan and Saudi Arabia), has largely replaced Islamic law with Western-inspired legal revisions. The classifications of actions as crimes differs from classical shari'a, in which criminal law in the Western sense did not exist and the categorization of actions requiring societal sanctions differed.

In the Egyptian code there are two groups of crimes that involve women: First, there are crimes against honor, including acts that "violate the sexual freedom of individuals or offend their sense of sexual modesty" such as rape, sexual assault, indecent public exposure, adultery, and prostitution (Mohsen 1990, 17). The second category includes homicide, theft, and possession or sale of contraband. Recent research by Safia Mohsen on the Egyptian criminal code suggests that gender affects the judgments made in both categories of cases and that traditional conceptions of women work to women's disadvantage in some crimes, but to their advantage in others (Mohsen 1990). The court's examination of the circumstances and the motivation behind the crime seem to be vital in making the judgment. Here social mores come into play and, at times, a protective attitude toward women is displayed, while, in other cases, women are judged harshly for violating community and religious codes of conduct.

For example, infanticide is generally a crime committed by women. Since it contradicts common conceptions of women as nurturing mothers, law enforcement officials believe it is done more in ignorance than malice. Mohsen quotes a police officer: "No woman in her right mind would knowingly or voluntarily kill her own child even if it is an illegitimate child. Her punishment is in the loss of the child and the guilt over it. Any additional legal punishment does not serve the interest of anyone." (Mohsen 1990, 17–8). However, a mother who killed her six-month-old son as a means of punishing her husband for seeing another women was charged with murder and believed likely to be prosecuted to the full extent of the law (Mohsen 1990, 18).

Judgments for homicide include punishments for women. In the code, six conditions (e.g., the use of poison in committing murder) are cited whereby murder would carry the death penalty. Women seem to be marked for severe punishment as they favor poisoning over other weapons, some of which may not qualify for the death penalty. The reasoning of legal authorities takes another tack. They argue that poisoning is included in that list as it is a particularly reprehensible crime that permits no warning for the victim. Also, the crime often represents betrayal by a close friend or relative who poisons the victim's food and may claim other lives than the one intended (Mohsen 1990, 18).

The law on homicide by provocation, notably when linked to adultery, also discriminates. A man who kills his adulterous wife and/or her partner—catching them in the act—is punishable with a maximum sentence of six months in prison (Article 237 of the Penal Code). If a woman surprises her husband in like circumstances and kills him, she is charged with murder. Here, provocation changes the legal description of the crime. The reasoning for this discrepancy refers back to Islamic law. Since a husband can marry a second wife, a wife should not be unduly upset if she discovers him in adultery, as he has an inherent right to relations with another woman. However, the husband has exclusive right to his wife's body (Mohsen 1990, 19). This argument is similar to that employed in shari'a for rulings on hadd punishments for adultery.

Punishment for adultery brings up gender-based divergent penalties based on the same reasoning. The penalty for an adulterous husband is six months, for a woman it is two years. Men and women also differ in their right to claim a crime. A husband can charge his wife with adultery no matter where she commits the crime. A woman may only charge her husband with adultery if he is caught with his partner in the family residence.

Charges of rape usually result in negative consequences for the woman. It is difficult to prove rape; women claiming rape are considered adulterers and can be punished as such. Most hesitate to bring charges or to let their families know of a violation or attempted violation. The major question to establish is the woman's lack of consent. If that can be settled, violators are punished at hard labor. If the offender is a member of her immediate family, someone with authority over her, someone entrusted with her care or supervision or a domestic in her service, the term is increased to life at hard labor. Rape is defined as a crime committed only against women. Part of the rationale behind the stringent punishment is that rape violates the sexual rights of the husband and the reputation of the victim's family. Attempted rape may be charged in cases where the assault was interrupted (Mohsen 1990, 20–1).

In other crimes, such as theft and drug dealing, women are often dealt with more leniently than men. The logic of enforcement agencies seems to be that women are less capable of taking care of themselves, and society has the responsibility to care for them. More likely, when a woman commits a crime, it is more through ignorance and lesser mental capacity than through iniquity. Thus, the woman is less responsible for her actions and deserves more lenient punishment. Women are exempted by law from serving in hard-labor camps for crimes that specify that punishment. Women with small children are allowed to have their children with them in prison if no adult relative is willing to care for the children (Mohsen 1990, 22–3).

Many of the judgments and sentences reflect social mores that take a distinctive view of women. Parallels to the attitudes spelled out above can be found in traditional Islamic law and in customary practice of many Muslim communities.

Muslim Arguments on Women's Status

The most important question that governs legal reforms is who interprets Islam? Other questions could be added: Who interprets or lays out the position of Islam on women? Should traditionally trained Muslim clerics interpret Islam in regard to women's status? Should individual Muslims who read and ponder scripture, such as the women members of activist groups, interpret women's roles in Islam? Should Muslim scholars trained in the methodologies of both the West and the Muslim sciences interpret Islam in this regard? Should men and women who live their lives as righteous Muslims determine what Islamic precepts on women's status should be? Should the governments of nation-states and the judges who interpret national law have the task of interpreting Islam? Answers depend on whom you ask. Increasing levels of education allow Muslims access to sources to determine their own positions on religious matters. Islam does not recognize an intermediary between believers and God. Believers must have sufficient education to read the Qur'an, hadith, and other religious sources.

Various approaches to the status of women in Islamic law have developed. Each stems from a particular conception of Islam and from the methodology used in working out the position. Differences in dealing with hadith are key to the differences among the schools of law and among the following groups. Focus on the Qur'an, as the point of departure for legal reasoning, has been emphasized by Muslim reformers over the past millennium. This section discusses four groups currently enmeshed in an ongoing debate: traditional Muslims; Islamists, or Muslim activists; Muslim reformers (modernists), including Muslim feminists; and, finally, Muslim secularists. Many lines blur, and opinions overlap.

Despite similarities, the above groups differ considerably in their position on women and family and in the often not fully developed methodologies they use to arrive at those positions. This section looks at the different ways Muslims work out positions on women from Islamic sources. Alternatively, it shows how they may choose to reject Islamic sources and substitute another basis of reasoning.

A larger question being considered is how the Qur'an is to be read and interpreted as successive centuries bring changes in the situations of Muslims. The latter twentieth century has brought renewed study and debate over the practice of *ijtihad*, or independent reasoning, that has opened religious texts to discussion. The science of Islamic jurisprudence is based on alternative emphases and readings that allow different interpretations. Have traditional readings and exegesis of Qur'anic passages been correctly determined? How much does the explanation or exegesis of a particular verse reflect the attitudes of the commentator? Are there alternate readings of Qur'anic verses that deserve attention? Whose exegesis of a given passage should be accepted? How does one read the Qur'an fifteen centuries after it was revealed? Does the life lived by those reading the Qur'an influence their interpretation of its text? Should not the Qur'anic principles of equality before God and socioeconomic justice guide the interpretation of other verses? If so, do we arrive at different readings of the material? To what extent did the male-dominated patriarchal background of the Arabs influence the context of Islamic legal prescriptions? How much did community practice bias legal judgments of Maliki, Hanafi, Shafi'i, and Hanbali jurists?

Similar hermeneutical and critical questions are receiving serious scholarly attention in schools of textual criticism worldwide. For Muslims, questions concerning core practices of Islam in the twenty-first century are of paramount importance. For scholars and community leaders attempting to answer these questions, both the condition of women and how women are addressed by family law present difficult situations.

The question widens under examination to include scrutiny of other sources of Islamic law. Individual hadith texts have been attacked for centuries as attempts to manipulate legal conclusions. Scholars have long been concerned with the science of determining correct hadith. Muslim reformers question hadiths that contradict what they believe to be the spirit of the Qur'an.

Islamists (Muslim activists) and Muslim reformers (modernists) distrust the framework of Islamic jurisprudence that developed over the centuries and question whether it reflects devotion to traditional practice and non-Qur'anic sources more than it represents the word (Islamist view) or spirit (reformer view) of the Qur'an. Other approaches question the applicability of a seventh-century document to the changing needs of contemporary society.

TRADITIONAL MUSLIM POSITIONS

Traditional Muslims view Islam as a revealed way of life that encompasses both faith and doctrine. Islam's sources are the Qur'an, the hadith texts, and community consensus (*ijma'*) of Muslim jurists; the center of Islam is the shari'a. Islamic law is an elaborate edifice of scripture-based analysis that derives from these three sources and is expressed in the body of fiqh, jurisprudence literature that has been compiled over the past fourteen centuries. Considerable differences of opinion have been recorded in the Islamic legal texts over time, but all derive from the same basis of legal reasoning. Although the schools of law differ in some regards, they all respect the findings of the other schools.

Traditional Muslims accept some adaptation of traditional approaches to the concerns of a given period. Their methods involve building consensus and reworking juridical reasoning, working within set institutions, perhaps emphasizing one ethical principle or legal category over another. Although not inflexible, their process takes time and is built upon traditional sources. Included in the process are traditionally educated professors of Islamic studies and officials in ministries of Islamic affairs ('ulama). Although their numbers have shrunk over the course of this century, their influence has remained strong as spokespersons for Islam. Many religious scholars today are closely tied to state interests, either through their lobbying efforts, their work in state ministries, or their close association with state-funded educational institutions or state-run mosques.

Traditional Muslims emphasize respect for women and for a woman's role as wife and mother. They stress, however, the different positions fulfilled by men and women in society: the men in the workplace and the women in the domestic sphere. While not denying that women are socially and legally inferior, they assert that men and women are, in fact, equal. This equality is based on immutable differences between the sexes; men and women are seen as separate but equal.

Earlier in this century, Muslim writers argued the superiority of men over women, as part of God's order requiring that women be submissive to men. Egyptian nationalist leader Tal'at Harb wrote, "Women were created for men's earthly pleasures and in order to take care of domestic affairs; God did not create them to attempt to defeat the men, nor to give opinions or establish policies." (Stowasser 1987, 269).

Muhammad Kamil al-Fiqi, former dean of the Faculty of Arabic and Islamic Studies at al-Azhar, stated:

> Women were created constitutionally different from men. The heart of the female weighs only four-fifths of that of the man (at birth), her respiratory organs are weaker, and Western science has furthermore established that the average weight gain of the female infant is less than that of the male. In constitution and physique, women resemble children. Like children, they are emotional and lacking analytic insight, are given to unbalanced mood shifts, from joy to sorrow, from pain to pleasure, from hatred to love. (Stowasser 1987, 270).

Muhammad Abdul Rauf, a former professor at al-Azhar and former head of the Islamic Center in Washington D.C., is a well-respected theologian and scholar. His position can be taken as a fair statement of traditional Islamic doctrine expressed in light of the gender wars of the late twentieth century. In his book, *The Islamic View of Women and the Family*, he presents a carefully modulated thesis on the place of women in Islam that lays out a moderate position on the status of women but which adheres carefully to traditional sources and reasoning. In this book, Abdul Rauf declares that men and women are equal in Islam but then carefully argues that this equality does not rule out different functions and responsibilities.

> Thus is the status of women under the law of Islam. It is a status to which a woman is entitled as a basic right, but of which she had been deprived by ages of social and historical prejudices and injustices until it was restored to her by Islam. Under this just status,
>
> As a mother, a woman is to be treated with filial love and veneration,
>
> As a daughter, she is to be treated with parental love and compassion,
>
> As a sister, she is to be treated with devoted love, respect and consideration,
>
> As a wife, she is to be treated with constant concern, unbounded care, deep sympathy and loving passion,
>
> And outside these family ties, just simply as a woman, she is:
>
> An individual worthy of dignity and respect,
>
> An independent human being,
>
> A social person,
>
> A legal person,
>
> A responsible agent,
>
> A free citizen,
>
> A servant of God, and
>
> A talented person, endowed, like a male person, with heart, soul and intellect; and has a fundamental equal right to exercise her abilities in all areas of human activities. (Abdul Rauf 1977, 29)

In the next chapter, Abdul Rauf begins, "Although men and women are equal, they are somewhat different." Differences include different reproductive systems, different physiological functions. "Men ejaculate, women menstruate. Men inseminate and women conceive and lactate" (31). Abdul Rauf then builds his argument on the differences and similarities. He notes that the differences between men and women do not mean that women cannot undertake many of the same functions as men, to work, to trade, to teach, to preach, to receive equal rewards for tasks women carry out in the same way men carry them out. He carefully states that a woman's religious obligations are the same as a man's. The obstruction of women's rights are due to local practices and customs, not to the strictures of Islam.

The differences, however, are decisive:

> Yet, sex differences are reflected in certain areas; namely, in granting women some religious concessions in certain situations, in laying greater emphasis on feminine modesty, and in the most crucial pattern of conjugal relationship.
>
> ... Equality means equal entitlement to human dignity, to respectful treatment, to free choice and freedom of action. It is equality before God and before the law. It is equality of religious and moral responsibility. Domestic sex roles, on the other hand, have to provide certain functional diversities arising from the natural sex differences which are not at all inconsistent with that sense of equality. ... Attaching greater value to one of these reciprocal functions over the other is arbitrary and unjustified. Therefore, sex role differences should not imply a sense of inferiority or superiority to one party over the other (Abdul Rauf 1977, 37–8).

Abdul Rauf reasons that distribution of duties and functions among members of a group must take abilities and differences among respective members into consideration to promote smooth functioning. Not to do so would be irresponsible as well as inefficient. When the status or function of a task has nothing to do with the sex of an individual, as in the case of a schoolteacher, then male and female roles can be similar. This is not the case for a husband and wife where the roles they play in a family are complementary and reciprocal. Even if the interest of the group calls for inequality of authority, there is no reason for value judgments of inferiority or superiority.

Abdul Rauf's analysis emphasizes that, although the man is the head of the house, he is not to make decisions arbitrarily or to behave tyrannically. His use of key words, reciprocal and complementary, refers to his view of the place of women and men in Islamic law—working together for the well-being of the family unit. In much of his reasoning, Abdul Rauf differs little from the conservative modernists in his willingness to reform patently unjust practices arising from Islamic law—for instance, to give the woman the right of consent in her marriage and allowing custody decisions to be made in the best interests of the children, which often means leaving them with the mother.

A woman's right to property ownership is steadfastly defended. In every possible variation on the theme of property, right to credit, and right to manage property without consent or knowledge of her husband or male guardian, spokespersons support the right to individual control over property and the right to inherit (although the share of inheritance may be less than a man in the same position in the family).

The dictum that two women witnesses are needed in the place of one man stems from a Qur'anic verse speaking of financial transactions. "Get two witnesses out of your own men, and if there are not two men, then a man and two women, such as ye choose, for witnesses, so that if one of them errs, the other can remind her" (Qur'an 2:282). The verse means that women who are less familiar with contract law and financial negotiations than men may forget the procedure or be mistaken; therefore, two are needed, one to aid the other. This has been extrapolated to conclude that the testimony of a woman is of less value than that of a man and that it is un-Islamic for women to be involved in financial or business affairs.

Traditional Muslim stands vary from the modernists on one important point, the question of women's participation in public life and her right to work. The literature of traditional Muslims generally emphasizes the importance of women remaining in the home. Leaving the home to work brings up the potential disintegration of communal order. The woman away from her home and her male relatives is regarded as *fitna*, the source of social anarchy. She stands in danger of losing her chastity and her reputation, and she gives up far more than she gains (Stowasser 1987, 272). The Qur'an and hadith are read to forbid a woman's mixing with strange men, thus she is forbidden to work outside her home. Working women destroy conjugal and family order by challenging men's guardianship over women. They also endanger Muslim society by postponing marriage and child rearing to work.

Equally if not more harmful is the issue of women's participation in public policy formation. First, Islam directs that women are not to hold positions of community leadership. A hadith of Bukhari states, "A people who have appointed a woman to be their ruler will not thrive" (Stowasser 1987, 273). Women's access to political power brings up questions of democracy, equality, and freedom, and it questions the political and social order of Islamic society. Abdul Rauf, in warning Muslim women against the excesses of Western feminist movements, nowhere calls for political action to correct injustices, although he recognizes a variety of local problems and impediments to women's rights. Each part of the Muslim world, he says, seeks progress as suits its people, traditions, and background; each particular path of progress will engender its own distinct problems as trade-offs (Abdul Rauf 1977, 147).

Stowasser translates the text of a speech by Dr. Muhammad Yusuf Musa that lays out the conflicts engendered by the term "democracy."

We want to discuss the defects of the supporters of women's right to political candidacy, by which we mean democracy, equality and freedom, which allegedly should belong to everybody. There is a fine line between freedom and anarchy, which we must strive to preserve, as otherwise disaster will follow. Democracy and equality do not consist in the fact that everybody obtains what he wants at the expense of religion and the common weal; rather, they consist in general rights and duties ... which prevent that people oppress each other, and through which each citizen can confidently obtain the wages of his labor for which he is qualified in terms of nature, abilities and talents.

This democracy and the equality and freedom that go with it, do not empower each citizen to obtain any work he desires, no matter how insignificant.

Dr. Musa emphasizes the Qur'anic teaching that men are not created equal in nature, talent, ability, and qualification: "It is We Who portion out between them their livelihood in the life of this world: and We raise some of them above others in ranks ..." (Qur'an 43:32). To clinch his argument concerning barring women from political life, he cites: "And women shall have rights similar to the rights against them, according to what is equitable: but men have a degree over them" (2:228).

These questions of women in political life and the definition and understanding of democracy and equality are part of a wide-ranging political debate, which is destined to rage for some time. The vehemence of the debate and the issue of women as a component in a democratic order illustrate the force of some of these questions. Some spokespersons for this position even recommend the intervention of the state to enforce private morals and declare that it is the duty of the state as well as the community at large to force the woman to save herself—in terms of her morality, physical well-being, and reputation by forcing her to return to domestic life even if it means paying her a pension (Stowasser 1987, 272).

In taking on these questions of democracy, for which there are equally compelling uses of scripture by prodemocracy forces, traditional Muslims (with their close ties to state institutions and power centers) tread on shaky ground. Their methods require establishing scriptural (Qur'anic and hadith) bases for law, searching for like situations in the jurisprudence texts, and seeking to preserve and strengthen Muslim interests. A major problem is doing so in a rapidly secularizing world.

MUSLIM ACTIVIST OR ISLAMIST GROUPS

Here we will define Muslim activists, or Islamists, as individuals who actively utilize Islam in the political sphere. Many wish to see Islamic law as the basis of government. A major difference between traditional Muslims scholars and activists is their methodology. Islamists, or Muslim activists, see the sources of Islam—the Qur'an and, secondarily, the Sunna (Prophet Muhammad's actual practice within the Muslim community, which was recorded in the hadith texts)—as unchanging and immutable. Islam, as the final revelation, lays out an absolute truth, valid for all times and places. Islam defines social reality rather than being shaped by or responding to it. As many of the jurisprudence texts could be read as attempts to interpret or adapt Islamic law to social needs or historical variables, Islamists tend to dismiss this body of law as insufficiently close to scriptural meaning or as owing too much to local customs to the detriment of religious strictures. They prefer to cut straight to the Qur'an and the hadith texts and reason from that point. Their methodology differs greatly from the traditional Muslim position but parallels that of the modernists.

The sense that things have gone badly awry in the Muslim world is integral to their thought. Muslims must backtrack and root out practices antithetical to Islam that are poisoning Muslim society. These deadly practices include Western-influenced political orders and social impurities—cabarets, prostitution, adultery, illegitimate children, AIDS, professional women so hardened that their reproductive organs no longer function to conceive children. To remedy the situation, certain institutions must be restored. A major priority is family order, which is the cornerstone of Muslim community. The role of women becomes a basic signal of the social order or its lack. Other Islamist issues include the ban on bank interest, ban on family planning, collection of zakat (tithes), and enmity to the Zionist state of Israel, all of which distinguish Islam from the West.

On women's roles, the Islamist and traditional Muslims emphasize woman's natural domesticity, her God-given role as mother and wife, the physical differences that separate her from man, the respect owed her in Islam. They also believe that chaos and destruction of the Muslim community will follow changes in women's activities, particularly, the entry of women into the world of public affairs.

To the Islamist, however, the villain in this scenario is the imperialist West—seen as all Western interests and their stooges: governments and media, financial, and development agencies. This latest attack upon Islam takes place on the battlefield of the family unit, as Western notions of women's liberation and the realization of the individual are antithetical to Islamic views of women and family. The Islamists consider local women's liberation movements that sprang up in various Muslim countries to be deviant innovations resulting from backwardness and ignorance among Muslims. If Muslim women truly understood their religion, their society, and their place in it, there would be no support for these Western aberrations.

The West, however, has mounted an all-out attack, similar in scope and intensity to earlier military campaigns. Tools in their strategy are the introduction into Muslim countries of policies that allow women in the workplace, immodest clothing for women, reform in family law that restricts polygamy and makes divorce available for women, allow women to take public positions, and so on. Foreign ideologies such as Zionism, Marxism, psychoanalytic theory (Freudianism), evolutionism, and existentialism are all condemned. Islamists defend polygamy as a preferable alternative to the West's prostitution and adultery; they defend early marriage (arranged by the family) as better than a young woman being forced to sell herself on the streets of America to find a husband.

Zaynab al-Ghazali terms herself the mother of the Muslim Brotherhood, for reasons of both her age and her seniority in the movement. She headed the Egyptian Muslim Women's Association in the early days of the Muslim Brotherhood, has been a key member of the Islamist groups, and has campaigned for better scriptural education of women. Although Islamist groups may recommend limits to the scope of women's activities in the public sphere, they emphasize the importance of education to better defend one's rights in Islam. As a result, religious associations have women's sections; most mosques sponsor Qur'anic lessons for women. In line with their belief that the Muslim woman is key to a true Muslim society, Islamists have emphasized the role of Muslim women in the family and the importance of a sound family to a virtuous community.

Al-Ghazali is an interesting model for Muslim women. She divorced her first husband because his emphasis upon domesticity took up all her time and took her away from her mission with the Muslim Brotherhood. Her second husband gave her written agreements that he would not come between her and her mission but would help her and be her assistant. Within these bounds, they shared cooperation, love, faithfulness to God, and purity of soul and conscience, and they were only separated when she was sent to prison (under the Nasser regime).

In keeping with her own career, al-Ghazali holds that Islam does not forbid a woman from participating in public life, entering into politics, or expressing her opinion, as long as those activities do not interfere with her first duty as a mother. If she has free time, she may participate in activities outside the home. Al-

Ghazali's views on this subject are not completely supported by other spokespersons for Islamist movements (Hoffman 1985).

In reality, Islamist women are found not only in the home; many are students and young working women; many engage in political activity. The choice to wear Islamic dress is a statement announcing that here is a responsible, respectable Muslim woman who is not to be bothered. In other words, her dress (like the veil in some situations) becomes a badge of respectability that shields her from improper advances.

Muslim activists have directly challenged the modern Islamic reform of family law. They hold that state-sponsored reforms in personal status law should be revoked. Khomeini's Islamic Republic repudiated Iran's Family Protection Act. Conservative Islamists in Pakistan have called for the repeal of the Muslim Family Laws Ordinance. Muslim activist groups in Egypt, the Sudan, Libya, Pakistan, Mauritania, Algeria, and Tunisia have inveighed against reforms in family law and have called for a return to the shari'a as the source of law.

Islamist statements on areas that concern women include the following. Polygamy is allowed, and no restrictions on its practice can be legislated by the state or written into marriage contracts. Divorce lies in the hands of the husband, and no reforms should interfere with his right to repudiation. Veiling (*hijab*) and/or modest dress for women is required by the Qur'an. Family-planning measures are antithetical to Islamic doctrine in that they confound the actualization of God's will. A conservative approach to the position of women in Islam has become a critical criterion for determining one's religious correctness.

The concern of the Muslim activists is to establish a strong Islam that will allow Muslims and Islam to take a leading place in world, bring Muslims back to true practice of Islam, and ordain practices that guarantee socioeconomic justice for all Muslims.

MUSLIM REFORMERS OR MODERNISTS

Muslim intellectuals and writers in the latter nineteenth century worked at countering what they saw as stagnation besetting Islam and Muslim countries. Determined that Islam had been limited by conservative jurists who relied too heavily on precedents and tradition, they sought to establish a new methodology for determining contemporary issues by reasoning from original sources of Islam. This movement is referred to as the *salafiyya*, and primary figures include Muhammad Abduh and Rashid Rida. These men saw early Islam as the manifestation of pure religion and believed that, in subsequent years, developments that departed from this pure Islam sullied its principles and practices. In the course of their work, they dismissed all but the Qur'an and some Sunna and hadith as binding.

In the absence of guidance from the Qur'an and Sunna, modernists applied ijtihad, or independently derived legal reasoning. Reworking the legal bases for social practices granted them latitude to achieve some of their goals. Modernists would say that while the conservative Muslims regard the Qur'an to be a law book, reformers see the Qur'an as the religious source of the law. The Qur'an, then, contains the principles of religion that then can be applied to the exigencies of each time and place. This flexibility and adaptability were regarded with concern by traditional conservative Muslims. They saw not flexibility but heresy in this adaptability and feared divisiveness as each community began constructing its own Islam and abandoned the uniformity found in adherence to traditional modes of jurisprudence.

Modernists attempt to isolate timeless principles of Qur'anic doctrine and Islamic law and then extrapolate from them legally permissible social practices. They see Islam as a dynamic living religion. This dynamism issues from the doctrines espoused in the Qur'an, which are applicable worldwide and throughout time. Using this Qur'anic blueprint, men and women trained in Islamic precepts may rework social practices to the needs of a given community. Social practices, as opposed to religious practices, which are unchanging, should respond to practical needs of a given generation and locale. Many of the principles worked out by these reformers became the basis for family-law reforms.

Reexamination of Muslim sources has become a standard exercise over the past century for intellectuals and social thinkers, as well as Muslim theologians who wish to examine the possibilities of reform while still operating well within the Muslim tradition. Muslim reformers begin with education for women, which they strongly advocate as the basis of reform. Reformers hold that since women are the spiritual and intellectual equals of men, women have an absolute right to an education, to participate in public life, and to work outside the home. A prominent modernist, Mahmud Shaltut (d. 1963) as Rector of al-Azhar University, opened that bastion of Islamic learning and tradition to women, although they studied different subjects on a different campus.

In family-law reform, modernists emphasize a woman's right to choose a marriage partner. Some modernists consider polygamy a destructive custom that should be abolished. They hold that although polygamy was important in the early Muslim community when practiced properly, it was abused by later generations of Muslims who employed it to satisfy lust. Others, although unwilling to abolish polygamy, felt that it should be severely limited and only allowed by judicial decision. The rationale behind allowing polygamy stemmed from the principle of *istislah*, or taking public interest into account. Cases where this would apply would include a barren wife or where a Muslim community might legislate the practice when it felt it suited to the community's needs.

Modernists recognize that the practice of divorce holds abuses for women. To rectify these problems, they recommend greater rights for women to initiate divorce—along the lines of the Maliki school's use of khul'. Male rights to divorce need to be institutionalized and regulated by a judicial hearing and granted by a judge. As women granted allegiance (*bay'a*) to the Prophet

Muhammad, women hold the right of political participation. Modernists generally reject the (hijab) veil and its connotations of seclusion and sexual segregation for women. They cite the Qur'an as requesting modesty in dress for both sexes, not only women.

Although modernists do not rework or rethink the concept of patriarchal structure in Islam, they attempt to redress what they see as inequities in the law. They hold that man's superiority over women (Qur'an 2:228, 4:34) has been interpreted incorrectly. The meaning of the verses is limited and only concerns man's status as head of the family. As the family must be organized, the man's responsibility is to provide for the family. The woman's role is to be in charge of domestic affairs.

Temporary stumbling blocks to the reformers have included scriptures that indicate that despite declarations of equality, in practice women are not considered competent. The scripture necessitating two women witnesses in the place of one man is a case in point. The reformers work through this verse in a different manner than traditional Muslims. They begin by establishing the general rule, the equality of men and women, then move to the specific case—financial transactions. They reason that two women were mandated in the place of one man because, as the verse implies, being unfamiliar with business matters, a woman may err and need another's help. The solution of the modernists is not to ignore the principle of equality between men and women but to transform the specific case, thus allowing the equality spoken of in the Qur'an. The final postulate would be that women should be more fully involved in financial matters so they are prepared to be competent witnesses with expertise equal to that of men (Rahman 1980, 48–9).

Islamic modernists were heavily influenced by Western mores, practices, and legal codes in working through their approaches to social issues. One modernist stated: "The more the East imitates the West, the better off it will be; to speak of European morality as 'corrupt' and of Islamic civilization as 'spiritually superior' is

merely wishful thinking, the revenge of the impotent, a 'lullaby'"
(Qasim Amin quoted in Stowasser 1987, 265).

The modernists have had a decisive impact on reform of family law, especially in expanding the rights of women. However,
other modernists who called for further work on the subject
criticized their methodology of reform for not being sufficiently
systematic. Others criticized their approach for not being sufficiently far-reaching. The Islamists distrust modernists, seeing
them as lackeys of the West seeking to destroy Islam from the
inside. Traditional jurists condemned their attempts to rethink
legal strictures pertaining to women and family matters. In the
debate over family-law reform in Pakistan, traditional Muslims
dismissed modernist attempts at reform in scathing terms.

> [T]o take personal and individual whims as the basis for the deriva-
> tion of laws and principles is neither fiqh nor ijtihad but amounts to
> distorting the religion of God and the worst type of heresy. In spite
> of their blatant departure from the view of the Muslim commenta-
> tors and jurists, no member of the Commission could take the place
> of Fakhruddin Razi or Abu Hanifa. This is the reason that certain
> recommendations, which reflect subservience to the West of some of
> the members and their displeasure with Islam, constitute an odious
> attempt to distort the Holy Qur'an and the sunna with a view to
> giving them a Western slant and bias. . . . (Esposito 1982b, 205)

MUSLIM FEMINISTS

Female Muslim critics of Muslim stances on women's status have
generally supported the reformers' attempts, although they may
call for wider applications and wider scope of reform. The feminists, like the reformers, base their reforms on Islamic sources. A
subcategory of scholars, progressive Muslim feminists, supports
this method of expanding Islam's position on women. They call
for a reexamination and reworking of Islamic texts dealing with
the position of women.

Works that reason from this departure point include those

of Freda Hussain, Aziza al-Hibri, Nawal al-Saadawi, Khaled Abou El Fadl, and Fatima Mernissi, whose book, *The Veil and the Male Elite*, summarizes this methodology well. Amina Wadud, in *Qur'an and Woman: Rereading the Sacred Text from a Woman's Perspective*, applies ijtihad to Qur'anic verses on women and re-works traditional pronouncements and conventional approaches. These and other works by Muslim women criticize the traditional Muslim position on women from the standpoint of a faithful Muslim woman. Through careful analysis, they question traditional readings of the Qur'an and Islamic legal texts that limit women's rights. Much of their work points out the influence of historical attitudes—both within Arab and Muslim culture and outside of it—in formulating practices believed integral to Islam, such as veiling (hijab) and seclusion of women. Aziza al-Hibri phrases their major question: "There is no doubt that Islamic tradition and culture is patriarchal. But the important question is whether Islam, as revealed through the Qur'an, is patriarchal" (al-Hibri 1982, viii).

Muslim feminists challenge traditional readings of scripture, the veracity of hadith, and historical stereotypes of women to force a reevaluation of the place of women within Islam. Their scholarship, which uses textual reading and historical evaluation, goes beyond the scope of the reformers. Feminists call for supporting reforms already made, as well as for further reform, to bring legal statutes and social practices that concern women in line with the expressions of equality in the Qur'an.

Women writing as Muslim feminists hold a strategic political advantage. This stems from their status as Muslim believers within the Islamic tradition. They are thereby able to criticize the status quo and call for reform from a position of greater strength as a faithful Muslim, rather than alienating themselves, as do many anti-Muslim feminists and secularists.

The term "Muslim feminist" is not accepted by all of these scholars. Many hold that feminism is a Western construct with pejorative meanings of individualism and lack of concern for the family unit. Muslim feminists insist that women's equal status is consistent with Islam. However, family and community are central to their concerns.

SECULARISTS

Secularists are not statistically significant, but they are well represented in government policymaking and socioeconomic development and include many intellectuals. Although the majority of secularists are Muslim, they draw a distinction between religious affairs and public issues. This encompasses positions that separate the religious sphere from the political sphere (a view generally held by Muslims working within the framework of political secularism generated by Western political thought). This train of thought does not recognize secularism as antireligious or atheistic. Rather, institutionalized religion remains outside the political structure and stipulates autonomy for religion through its noninvolvement in politics. A model is the United States' separation of church and state.

One example of such secularism in the Islamic world is Turkey, where Islam was removed from the constitution in 1928 as the culmination of Ataturk's reforms. With this move, Turkey abolished its traditional system of religious law and courts and substituted institutions derived from the Swiss Civil Code. However, Turkey went further than did the United States, for it abolished religion from the public sphere while the United States prevented any establishment of religion as dominant and gave all religions similar rights. Other nations, namely Tunisia, South Yemen, and prerevolutionary Iran, have introduced revisions of their personal status codes. They have all reformed the system working from the traditional shari'a base, rather than denying the right of any religion to serve as the basis for law. Methodologically, these positions are akin to those elaborated by John Locke, Thomas Hobbes, and other Western figures, beginning with Martin Luther.

The historical process of reforming Muslim law codes gives support to the secularist position. The majority of Muslim nations substituted Western-derived codes of law for shari'a during the fifteenth through mid–twentieth centuries (exceptions: Saudi Arabia, Pakistan, and Libya). The one constant exception to this process has been the area of personal status law. Most of these nations retain a parallel system of courts, with shari'a courts to handle personal status procedures. Those who espouse departing from shari'a in the area of personal status law are advocating completion of a process well under way. Segments of society that resist dropping the Islamic basis of personal status law point to the importance of the family as the basis of society.

Many secularists do not advocate removing religion from the lives of Muslims; they would describe themselves as believing Muslims. For reasons of policy coherency and social justice, they recommend policies that separate the religious sphere from the political. A vital area of Islamic influence was breached earlier in this century with the secularization of traditional Islamic education systems. Whether religious scholars saw this process as necessary to strengthen their nations against colonialism or they were not powerful enough to mount a concerted attack, they did not resist the implementation of Western education programs.

Most conservative or Islamist Muslims would denounce the secularist stance as atheistic, but the denunciation is a matter of degree. Muslims have become reconciled to some aspects of secularism, such as the introduction of Western educational and technological methods, that they see as key to the advancement of Muslim countries. Traditional Muslims would argue that family is an area integral to Islam, while commercial treaties with Western nations are not. Islamists answer that all law in Muslim countries should be Islamic law (shari'a), and shari'a should be the law of the state if Muslims are to be correctly guided.

Islamic Law and Customary Practice

Customary practice is important for two reasons. First, the customary practice of a community is highly regarded in Islamic law as a legal source extraneous to Islam. Islamic authorities considered custom as holding the force of law. Custom often contributed significantly to shari'a judgments. Second, customs or practices of a given community weigh heavily in determining conduct. Local custom and what is Islamically legal are inextricably intertwined in many practices concerned with women's lives. Here custom and common assumptions about women may influence legal interpretations or individual assumptions of what is correct according to Islam.

Custom ('ada, 'urf) and its body of unwritten laws developed through generations of practice. It became incorporated into Islamic law through the procedures of the judges, the content of the hadith traditions, and the importance of ijma' (consensus) as a source of Islamic law, along with the Qur'an (Esposito 1982b, 127). When a judge found no texts in the Qur'an or hadith applicable to the problem before the court, he turned to the custom of the community. Through time, customary practice came to form a substantial part of Islamic law, partly through a process of gradual influence upon shari'a. Islamic law holds that all that is not forbidden is permitted. The Muslim community deems practices that differ from place to place acceptable; this gives customary practice authority.

Another reinforcement of customary law lies in Islamic acceptance of other legal traditions. This recognition of the viability of local custom was often a vital tool in assimilating foreign groups conquered by the Muslim armies and guaranteeing the groups' rights under Muslim rule. This emphasis facilitated the incorporation of Christian, Jewish, and other religious communities into the Muslim empire. This affirmation of local practices and law reduced potential friction between the Muslim victors and local communities.

In addition, Muslim respect for the People of the Book—Christians, Jews, and, later, Zoroastrians—allowed a tolerant approach to their practices. This approach was of particular importance in the area of personal status law because the inclination of the Muslim governments was to leave personal status matters in the hands of each religious community and interfere as little as possible. Marriage, divorce, and inheritance law for non-Muslims followed their own religiously ordained practices. Customary law also held good for other matters where local practice held precedence over Islamic law. For example, in North Africa, resolution of tribal problems followed Berber customary practice among the various tribal groups, rather than Islamic law.

Customary practices and attitudes derived from customary practices intrude upon the practice and enforcement of shari'a so that, at times, the interpretation of law owes as much to custom as to Islamic precepts. An example is equating the honor of the family with the honor of its women. This emphasis on female honor has colored many local practices of Islam (Abu-Lughod 1986). At the same time, women are seen as weaker and more vulnerable than men, and, thereby, need to be protected not only from other men, but also from their own instincts.

Customary practice and Islamic law often conflict in matters concerning natal family rights vis-à-vis conjugal (marital) family rights. The Islamic shift in emphasis toward the conjugal family is still challenged by family behavior. A striking example of this tension is found in both divorce and inheritance laws that see the wife as part of the husband's family, yet expect her to fall under the care of her natal family if problems such as divorce arise. A corollary of the inheritance law, which compensates women at one-half the rate at which men of equal degrees of relation are compensated, is that she always has recourse to the shelter of her natal family if deprived of her husband and left without a son.

THE BRIDE-PRICE AND PROPERTY RIGHTS

Another important case in point is that of the mahr, or bride-price, and women's right to property. Islamic law stipulates that the mahr belongs to the woman, not to her father or her husband, and grants her the right to hold and maintain her own property independently of her natal or marital family properties. Cases recorded by Richard Antoun in Jordanian courts demonstrated that the right of the woman to her mahr is often misunderstood by women. He tells of a woman who did not resist her father's claims to the mahr until the judge stated definitely that the mahr belonged to her to give to her father, to give to her husband, or to keep for herself. The judge here was in a quandary particular to his role. He had to determine which of two standards should be applied in this case, the customary practice—emphasizing natal family rights, especially the father's rights to the property of his family members—or the Islamic dictum that women may control their own property (Antoun 1990, 49–50). The Qur'an states, "And give unto the women [whom ye marry] free gift of their marriage portions; but if they of their own accord remit unto you a part thereof; then you are welcome to absorb it [in your wealth] (Qur'an 4: 4).

Another common trick played with the mahr is to declare a high mahr publicly and then specify another, lower mahr privately. The judge must decide which should be accepted. As the four schools of Sunni law differ on the resolution of this question, most judges consider all four positions and merge them with secular law, local custom, and the judge's own social philosophy (Antoun 1990).

In the Sudan, customary law and Islamic law conflict on the mahr, or bride-price. Custom is regularly reported as being more powerful than either shari'a or state law. Litigants who agree to, or are required to, place a case before the Shari'a Courts are surprised that Islamic law prevails. One case records a husband challenging his wife's possession of her total mahr on the basis of local custom that limits rights of a childless wife to the whole mahr. To his surprise, the court ruled along Qur'anic lines, judging that a mahr is an integral part of a Muslim marriage and the wife has the right of exercising total disposition of her property. As long as the husband recognized the validity of the marriage contract, the validity of the mahr was established (Fluehr-Lobban 1987, 14–6).

THE ISLAMIC HOME

Customary and Islamic values come into play over providing a proper "Islamic home" *(bayt shari'i)* for the bride. This Islamic emphasis upon the conjugal family unit as the basis of social values combines with traditional customary values such as modesty, privacy, and honor. Judges use the concept of an Islamic home, which recognizes the family unit in spatial and economic terms, as they struggle to determine if housing appropriate for a proper Muslim matron is provided. The traditional social values underlying a Muslim home—privacy and modesty, to which women are expected to adhere—also define a woman's honor (see Antoun 1990).

COURT SYSTEMS

Turkish women attempt to manipulate the dispensation of legal decisions by carefully calculating which court system—national courts, village councils, village headmen, or village mediators—will render a sympathetic opinion. Data show that women were far more likely than men to bring their cases to national courts; they file twice as many routine suits in the district courts and win more suits than men. By avoiding local justice systems that are more tied to Islamic practice and village custom, the women are less constrained by local interests. The local-level system is perceived as being more supportive to men, landowners, and senior citizens (Starr 1990).

Some Muslim states, such as Morocco and Iran, refer all cases of personal status to family courts that rule on family matters. Judges in these courts, especially in Morocco, may be women.

DIVORCE

Custom also plays into the life of Muslims in social controls over divorce. The right of the wife to apply for divorce is well established in the Sudan, but custom may cause her to hesitate to exercise this right. Settling a marital dispute in court is considered shameful, and to do so brings disgrace on the families. As the families of spouses often have close relations, an irresponsible divorce would harm both families and destroy those ties. As a result, the courts have worked out a method of circumventing these problems by appointing mediators to settle the dispute and recommend a course of action (Fluehr-Lobban 1987, 90–1). Mediation and reconciliation are important parts of the initiation of divorce in most Muslim countries, such as Iran, Iraq, and Turkey.

Abu-Lughod's work on the Bedouin of the Awlad Ali in Western Egypt notes that, despite Qur'anic reforms, blood ties remain strong between women and their natal families. Her research indicates that Islamic reworking of social organization into conjugal family units made few inroads in Awlad Ali territory. If religious law contradicts tribal custom, tribal custom reigns. In most cases, no contradiction is noted since most Awlad Ali hold that their tribal customs, moral code of honor, and Islamic law are indistinguishable.

Problems are solved, though, without recourse to law or outsiders (who would interpret or decide the law) except in case of great need. Abu-Lughod tells of women who resisted their husband's abuse by returning to their natal families and forcing their husbands to appease the women's kin if they wished their wives to return. In another case, a young woman resisted her father's wish that she marry her paternal cousin by feigning madness. In the end her parents brought her home, and when she came out of her seizure, they forced the groom's family to grant a divorce and return the bride-price. Abu-Lughod mentions that in extreme cases young men and women commit suicide in resistance to their fathers' wishes—especially in the case of marriage (Abu-Lughod 1986).

ECONOMIC SUPPORT

Islamic practices in sub-Saharan Africa illustrate some of the difficulties of blending custom with Islamic law. Despite Islamic rules that men are responsible for women's support, in reality, their contributions are relatively low. Women typically are responsible for their own and their children's upkeep with some assistance from their husbands. Men in Zambia resist modern ordinance marriage, as opposed to customary marriage, because it demands greater responsibility for care of their wives and children. For women, the trade-off is often made acceptable by gaining more autonomy from their husbands for their economic endeavors.

A study of secluded Hausa women in Kano suggests that although Islamic values define spatial arrangements and sexual division of labor, the women follow a West African pattern of autonomy and economic activity. This is achieved by utilizing their children to carry on the marketing of their products. A study done in Niger notes that the pre-Islamic matrilineal system exists alongside the nine-hundred-year-old Islamic system, mainly through the efforts of the women to preserve their separate rituals, their independent status, and a woman's vocabulary that excludes Arabic words (Kandiyoti 1991b, 28–31).

SEXUALITY

A theme that runs through popular beliefs is woman's extraordinary strength and attractiveness, which is sufficient to seduce men from their pious duties. This belief is tied to customary practice or popular folklore. The same images surface from time to time in religious writings. Fatima Mernissi writes that women are seen "as the embodiment of destruction, the symbol of disorder. She is *fitna*, the polarization of the uncontrollable, a living representative of the dangers of sexuality and its rampant disruptive potential" (Mernissi 1987, 13). Rampant sexuality, Mernissi holds, needs to be controlled. Through the Islamic institutions of marriage and family, this force is utilized for good, producing offspring and organizing society. Attempts to control women and subordinate their natural needs to the needs of a family are in the best interests of all.

WOMEN CONTROLLING WOMEN

The complicity of women in perpetuating practices that are against the interests of women can confuse outsiders. Older women often enforce practices that counter the desire of young women for greater autonomy. Female circumcision (clitoridectomy is the most common; more comprehensive forms exist) is a practice found along the Nile in the Sudan and Egypt and rarely in the Arabian Peninsula, the Levant, Iraq, and other parts of Africa. Although this practice has no Islamic sanction whatsoever, those who practice female circumcision attribute it to Islam and claim that good Muslim women should be circumcised. It grows out of the importance given to virginity (defined as an intact hymen) and is designed to curb a young woman's sexuality by reducing her desire for sexual intercourse. Many believe that circumcision enables a young girl to attract a husband. Although men in areas where female circumcision is practiced will defend it as a necessary practice and as an Islamic practice, women are responsible for performing the circumcision and perpetuating the practice—holding that good men expect a circumcised wife. Female circumcision is a key example of how customary practice must be distinguished from religiously mandated practice.

As women age, they gain power corresponding to their years of seniority in their household. Unless divorced or widowed without sons, their subordination to men is balanced by their increased power over younger women in the household. Their security in old age stems from the respect of their married sons and the labor and earning power of younger members of the household. Thus, to hold on to their newfound power, older women help perpetuate circumstances that, in their younger days, limited their own control.

The phenomenon of women seeking meaning in more traditional understandings of home and religion is not reserved for Islam. Research on fundamentalists aid our understanding of these forms of female action. Debra Kaufman, in *Rachel's Daughters: Newly Orthodox Jewish Women*, studies the return to Orthodox Judaism of U.S. women raised in Conservative or Reform Judaism. They consciously reject secular culture and the relativism of modern life, which they saw as a shallow and phony lifestyle. The women sought to reclaim domesticity, motherhood, and values of the female.

As Orthodox Judaism follows a strict delineation of male and female roles and places the woman firmly in the sphere of the home and family, these women turned from much of what they had known in their natal families to an overtly religious lifestyle. They found Orthodox Judaism a haven in a valueless world. The women returned to Orthodoxy wanting the certitude it offers. A sex-segregated world offers them great strength. However, Kaufman observes that with time and the growth of the newly Orthodox women's children, she expects to find them more involved in public ritual. She expects them to push the traditional boundaries set for Orthodox women, involving themselves more in religious study and developing the tools necessary to participate in their religious community (Debra Kaufman, personal communication, 11–13 March 1992).

VEILING

Veiling the face is one of the most well-known customary practices found in Islamic nations. Some Muslims claim that wearing a veil is mandatory as hijab, proper Islamic dress. A practice related to the veil is the seclusion of women. Muslims who support these practices cite the wives of the Prophet Muhammad who were enjoined to stay in their homes (Qur'an 33:33) and not to speak face to face with men not in the family (Qur'an 33:53), and they extrapolate these practices to all women. In reality the Qur'an asks the women simply to wear modest clothing and not to reveal their beauty to nonfamily members (Qur'an 33:59, 24:30–1). Practices related to veiling, to modest dress, and to the relatively new custom of Islamic dress are complicated social phenomena as much related to social and political factors as to religious convention. The practices differ among geographical locales, among socioeconomic classes, and over time.

Conclusion

The status of women in the Muslim world will remain a complex problem for some time to come. Part of the problem is the distinction between the theory and reality of male–female relations. Customary practice reveals discrepancies in the ways Muslims follow the prescriptions on women in Islamic law. A major concern of those who seek to reform Islamic law or to replace it with a code that guarantees equal rights to women is the breakdown of the system.

A crisis occurs when there is a disjunction between what was and what is, or between theory and reality—that is, when customary practice restricts rights already granted to women, negating the intent of Islamic law, or when personal error or misfortune interferes. For example, women have fallen through the cracks in Islamic law when they were orphaned, widowed, divorced, or deserted and then denied rights by their husband or help by their natal family; in other cases their men denied the tenets and spirit of the Islamic injunctions to treat women with kindness and fairness.

Islam imposed a revolutionarily different system upon the strongly patriarchal family structure of the pre-Islamic Arabs. Muhammad turned the emphasis of society from blood-ties to a community based on belief. In doing so, he also shifted emphasis from the natal family unit to the conjugal family unit. This change engendered tension that has not been fully resolved to this point and that accounts for conflicts in Muslim society.

Much of this tension stems from patriarchal custom warring with Islamic reforms or coloring interpretations of Islamic sources. This contradictory push and pull between the demands of a patriarchal society and the idea of equality of men and women, whether enumerated in the Qur'an or supplied by Western society, leads to conflicting views on the relations between men and women and the question of women's rights under the law.

Deniz Kandiyoti observes that it is at times when a traditional system falls into crisis that the antithetical forces that produced the crisis become visible. In this case, the traditional standards of behavior that Muslims had followed—whether in the Middle East, South and Southeast Asia, Africa, or the West—have been challenged by forces unleashed by modernization (Kandiyoti 1991b, 35). These include the impact of Western politics, economies, and other influences of globalization upon the Muslim world, the stresses of urbanization, the decline of the extended family, secularization, demographical pressures, and economic deprivation.

These simultaneous strains have stretched the system as far as it will go. The results unraveled the dominance of patriarchal custom by reducing the dependence of younger men on the older men of the family unit as the younger men move out of the family home and into their own, and by pushing women from the domestic sphere into public affairs and wage labor.

The increase of the contradictory forces attracted the attention of community guardians and provoked a variety of responses. Muslim reformers sought to rework Islamic legal methodology to yield judgments and practices closer to the principles of the Qur'an. Secularists replaced shari'a with Western law codes. Muslim activists (Islamists) defensively encircled their wagons around traditional readings of women's roles and castigated the West for the moral decay with which they contaminated the remainder of the world—specifically the Middle East. Muslim activists (and Muslim traditionalists) attempted to appease women by assigning them a high pedestal and emphasizing their place on the frontlines, defending Islam, home, and family against immoral outside forces.

Non-Muslims who read works about Muslim women or speak with them are justifiably confused by the variety of opinions. Some Muslim women inveigh against traditional or activist groups; others support policies that restrict women's options because they feel that attention equals concern and respect and assures female value. Farah Azari says that women in Iran support restrictive policies because the restrictions that the Islamic order placed on them were a "small price that had to be paid in exchange for the security, stability and presumed respect this order promised them" (Azari 1983, quoted in Kandiyoti 1991b).

The question of women's status precipitates another crisis: the very nature of Islam itself. Traditional Muslims hold that Islam is the way of life, that there are no distinctions between Islam and long-accepted practices, and that Islamic scriptures and law prescribe the role of women for all time. They are challenged by Muslim reformers and, in some ways, by Muslim activists. For the conservatives and activists, the question is not just the role of women in itself, but the role of women as a symbol of the validity of their type of Islam and their sense of community order. Part of the defensive posture of these stands stems from westernized Muslim society's definition of women in terms other than domestic.

The challenges to traditional Islamic conceptions of women and community have been profound. Secularists have eliminated

Islamic law and substituted Western statutes; reformers have reworked tenets of Islamic personal status law to bring it more in line with contemporary standards. These reforms are enormously threatening to conservative Muslims. The irony is that for many progressive Muslims, the reforms do not go far enough in ameliorating the situation of women.

Traditional Muslims maintain that Islam promotes equality between men and women; they would also note that men and women are different, but their differences do not negate their basic equality. Many Muslims are more comfortable describing the system as equitable. They believe that men and women have distinct roles assigned and distinct tasks that stem from their roles. The system supports each individual just as each individual contributes to it.

A problem arises when one ceases to talk of normative theoretical systems—ideal Islam—and confronts reality. When human frailty introduces injustice, one looks in the system to correct injustice and to keep the system equitable. But traditional Islamic law often lacks redress for victims of actions the Qur'an deplores. Attempts to equalize the position of the victim and the victimizer have been seen as attempts to tamper with revealed truth, not simply to address unforeseen flaws in jurisprudential interpretation and practice.

Bibliography

Abdul-Rauf, Muhammad. 1977. *The Islamic View of Women and the Family.* New York. Robert Speller and Sons.

Abou El Fadl, Khaled. 2001. *Speaking in God's Name: Islamic Law, Authority, and Women.* Oxford: Oneworld Publications.

Abu-Lughod, Lila. 1986. *Veiled Sentiments: Honor and Poetry in a Bedouin Society.* Berkeley: University of California Press.

———. 1993. *Writing Women's Worlds: Bedouin Stories.* Berkeley: University of California Press.

———. 1998. *Remaking Women: Feminism and Modernity in the Middle East.* Princeton, N.J.: Princeton University Press.

Abu Zahra, M. 1955. "Family Law." In *Law in the Middle East*, edited by M. Khadduri and H Liebesny. Washington, D.C.

Afkhami, Mahnaz, ed. 1995. *Faith and Freedom: Women's Human Rights in the Muslim World*. Syracuse, N.Y.: Syracuse University Press.

Ahmed, Leila. 1992. *Women and Gender in Islam*. New Haven: Yale University Press.

Alahyane, Mohamed, et al. n.d. *Portraits de femmes*. Casablanca: Editions le Fennec.

Al-Ali, Nadje. 2000. *Secularism, Gender and the State in the Middle East*. Cambridge: Cambridge University Press.

Antoun, Richard T. 1990. "Litigant Strategies in an Islamic Court in Jordan." In *Law and Islam in the Middle East*, edited by Daisy H. Dwyer. New York: Bergin and Garvey Publishers.

Azari, Farah, ed. 1983. *Women of Iran: The Conflict with Fundamentalist Islam*. London: Ithaca Press.

Beck, Lois, and Nikki Keddie. 1978. *Women in the Muslim World*. Cambridge: Harvard University Press.

Borraman, M. 1966. "Evolution of the Right of Repudiation and of Divorce." *Islamic Review* 54: 10.

Bowen, Donna Lee. 1980. "Islam and Family Planning in Morocco." *Maghreb Review* 5(1).

———. 1981. "Muslim Juridical Opinions Concerning the Status of Women as Demonstrated by the Case of 'Azl." *Journal of Near Eastern Studies* 40(4).

———. 1997. "Islam, Abortion, and the 1994 Cairo Population Conference." *International Journal of Middle Eastern Studies* 29(2): 161–84.

Combs-Schilling, M. Elaine. 1989. *Sacred Performances: Islam, Sexuality, and Sacrifice*. New York: Columbia University Press.

Coulson, Noel, and Doreen Hinchcliffe. 1978. "Women and Law Reform in Contemporary Islam." In *Women in the Muslim World*, edited by Lois Beck and Nikki Keddie. Cambridge: Harvard University Press.

Dallal, Ahmad. 1991. "The Islamic Institution of Waqf: An Historical Overview." Paper prepared for EMENA/EMTPH, World Bank, Washington, D.C. November 1991.

Dwyer, Daisy Hilse, ed. 1990. *Law and Islam in the Middle East*. New York: Bergin and Garvey Publishers.

El-Saadawi, Nawal. 1982. "Women and Islam." In *Women and Islam*, edited by Aziza Hibri. Oxford: Pergamon Press.

Esposito, John L. 1982a. *Women in Muslim Family Law*. Syracuse, N.Y.: Syracuse University Press.

————. 1982b. *Islam in Transition*. New York: Oxford University Press.

Esposito, John L., with Natana J. DeLong-Bas. 2001. *Women in Muslim Family Law*. Revised second edition. Syracuse, N.Y.: Syracuse University Press.

Fluehr-Lobban, Carolyn. 1987. *Islamic Law and Society in the Sudan*. London: Frank Cass and Co.

————. 1993 "Personal Status Law in the Sudan." In *Everyday Life in the Contemporary Middle East*, edited by D. L. Bowen and E. A. Early. Bloomington: Indiana University Press.

Fernea, Elizabeth W., ed. 1985. *Women and the Family in the Middle East*. Austin: University of Texas Press.

————. 1998. *In Search of Islamic Feminism: One Woman's Global Journey*. New York: Doubleday.

Fox-Genovese, Elizabeth. 1991. *Feminism without Illusions*. Chapel Hill: University of North Carolina Press.

Fyzee, Asaf A. A. 1974. *Outlines of Muhammadan Law*. Fourth edition. Delhi: Oxford University Press.

Gerhom, Tomas. 1985. "Aspects of Inheritance and Marriage Payment in North Yemen." In *Property, Social Structure, and Law in the Modern Middle East*, edited by Ann Mayer,. Albany: State University of New York Press.

Haddad, Yvonne Hazbeck. 1980. "Traditional Affirmations Concerning the Role of Women as Found in Contemporary Arab Islamic Literature." In *Women in Contemporary Muslim Societies*, edited by Jane Smith. Lewisburg, Penn.: Bucknell University Press; London: Associated University Presses.

Haeri, Shahla. 1989. *Law of Desire: Temporary Marriage in Shi'i Iran*. Syracuse, N.Y.: Syracuse University Press.

al-Hibri, Aziza, ed. 1982. *Women and Islam*. Oxford: Pergamon Press.

Hijab, Nadia. 1988. *Womanpower: The Arab Debate on Women at Work*. Cambridge: Cambridge University Press.

Hoffman, Valerie J. 1985. "An Islamic Activist: Zaynab al-Ghazali." In *Women and the Family in the Middle East: New Voices of Change*, edited by Elizabeth W. Fernea. Austin: University of Texas Press.

Hussain, Freda. 1984. *Muslim Women*. New York: St. Martin's Press.

Hussein, Aziza. 1985. "Recent Amendments to Egypt's Personal Status Law." In *Women and the Family in the Middle East: New Voices of Change*, edited by Elizabeth W. Fernea. Austin: University of Texas Press.

Kandiyoti, Deniz, ed. 1991a. *Women, Islam and the State*. Philadelphia: Temple University Press.

————. 1991b. "Islam and Patriarchy." In *Women in Middle Eastern History*, edited by Elizabeth W. Fernea. New Haven: Yale University Press.

————, ed. 1996. *Gendering the Middle East: Emerging Perspectives*. Syracuse, N.Y.: Syracuse University Press.

Karam, Azza M. 1997. *Women, Islamisms, and the State: Contemporary Feminisms in Egypt*. New York: St. Martin's Press.

Kaufman, Debra. 1991. *Rachel's Daughters: Newly Orthodox Jewish Women*. New Brunswick, N.J.: Rutgers University Press.

Lahrichi, Fadela Sebti Lahrichi. 1988. *Vivre musulmane au Maroc: Guide des droits et obligations*. Paris: Librairie Generale de Droit et de Jurisprudence.

Levy, Reuben. 1965. *The Social Structure of Islam*. Cambridge: Cambridge University Press.

Mannan, Muhammad Abdul. 1986. *Islamic Economics: Theory and Practice*. Revised edition. Boulder, Colo.: Westview Press.

Mernissi, Fatima. 1987. *Beyond the Veil*. Revised edition. Bloomington: Indiana University Press.

————. 1988. "Muslim Women and Fundamentalism." *Middle East Report* (July–August): 8–11.

————. 1991. *The Veil and the Male Elite: A Feminist Interpretation of Women's Rights in Islam*. Translated by Mary Jo Lakeland. Reading, Mass.: Addison-Wesley.

Mir-Hosseini, Ziba. 1993, 2000. *Marriage on Trial: A Study of Islamic Family Law*. London, New York: I. B. Tauris.

————. 1999. *Islam and Gender: The Religious Debate in Contemporary Iran*. Princeton, N.J.: Princeton University Press.

Mohsen, Safia K. 1990. "Women and Criminal Justice in Egypt." In *Law and Islam in the Middle East*, edited by Daisy H. Dwyer. New York: Bergin and Garvey Publishers.

Momen, Moojan. 1985. *An Introduction to Shi'i Islam: The History and Doctrines of Twelver Shi'ism*. New Haven: Yale University Press.

Moulay Rchid, A. 1985. *La Condition de la Femme au Maroc* Rabat: Edition de la Faculté des Sciences Juridiques Economiques et Sociales de Rabat.

Petry, Carl F. 1991. "Class Solidarity versus Gender Gain: Women as Custodians of Property in Later Medieval Egypt." In *Women in Middle Eastern History*, edited by Nikki Keddie and Beth Baron. New Haven: Yale University Press.

Rahman, Fazlur. 1980. *Major Themes of the Qur'an*. Minneapolis: Bibliotheca Islamica.

————. 1982. *Islam and Modernity*. Chicago: University of Chicago Press.

Royaume de Maroc. 1957. *Personal Status Code of Morocco*. Rabat: Official Bulletin no. 2378, 23 May 1958. Dahir no. 1–57–343, 28 Rab'i II, 1377 (November 22, 1957).

Sabbah, Fatna A. 1984. *Women in the Muslim Unconscious*. Translated by Mary Jo Lakeland. New York. Pergamon Press.

Schacht, Joseph. 1964. *An Introduction to Islamic Law*. Oxford: Clarendon Press, Oxford University Press.

———— 1990. "Mirath." *Encyclopedia of Islam*. Revised edition, vol. 7. Leiden: E. J. Brill.

Sonbol. Amira El Azhara, ed. 1996. *Women, the Family, and Divorce Laws in Islamic History*. Syracuse, N.Y.: Syracuse University Press.

Starr, June. 1990. "Islam and the Struggle over State Law in Turkey." In *Law and Islam in the Middle East*, edited by Daisy H. Dwyer. New York: Bergin and Garvey Publishers.

Stowasser, Barbara. 1984. "The Status of Women in Early Islam." In *Muslim Women*, edited by Freda Hussain. New York: St. Martin's Press.

————. 1987. "Liberated Equal or Protected Dependent? Contemporary Religious Paradigms on Women's Status in Islam." *Arab Studies Quarterly* 93.

————. 1994. *Women in the Qur'an, Traditions, and Interpretation*. New York and Oxford: Oxford University Press.

Toubia, Nahid, ed. 1988. *Women of the Arab World*. Translated by Nahed El Gamal. London: Zed Books Ltd.

Tucker, Judith. 1998. *In the House of the Law: Gender and Islamic Law in Ottoman Syria and Palestine*. Berkeley and Los Angeles. University of California Press.

White, Elizabeth H. 1978. "Legal Reform as an Indicator of Women's Status in Muslim Nations." In *Women in the Muslim World*, edited by Lois Beck and Nikki Keddie. Cambridge: Harvard University Press.

Wadud, Amina. 1999. *Qur'an and Woman: Rereading the Sacred Text from a Woman's Perspective*. Oxford: Oxford University Press.

3

Islamic Law and Family Planning

Donna Lee Bowen

The relationship between Islam and family planning is not clear cut. Religion often has a critical influence on a given culture's natality. Since the majority of the population of the Middle East and North Africa are Muslim, does Islam influence social mores that promote high birth rates and militate against use of family-planning measures? If so, what beliefs, teachings, and institutions are responsible? This paper examines Islam's contribution to factors that support or discourage use of family planning.

This subject lends itself to a larger question. To what extent is Islam a monolithic force and to what extent it is composed of diverse groups of believers with disparate positions? With over a billion Muslims dispersed from Brooklyn to Djakarta, does Islam have a central core that obliges believing Muslims to hold a given position on an issue? Or do local communities reason out their own understanding of religious questions?

Since the first century of Islam and the change in the rule of the Muslim community (*umma*) after the first four, "rightly guided" caliphs to the Umayyad dynasty, there has been no central Islamic rule, that is, no Muslim pope whose statements are binding for all Muslims. At various times, rulers with conflicting claims to legitimacy controlled different geographic areas from their capitals of Damascus, Baghdad, Cairo, and Cordova. These rulers were careful to legitimize their rule by adhering to Islamic values and by utilizing Islamic scholars (*'ulama*) to rule on legal questions. As the political rule by caliphs deteriorated into rule by strong princes with no personal claim to Islamic legitimacy, the welfare of the Islamic community was increasingly defended by the Muslim scholars in the most important Muslim schools and universities.[1]

After World War I, the Ottoman Empire, the last Muslim empire, was divided into separate nation-states. Currently, these states, plus others never part of the Ottoman Empire, are not ruled explicitly by Islamic law, although their populations are overwhelmingly Muslim. Exceptions are Saudi Arabia, Pakistan, and Iran, whose constitutions establish Islam as the foundation of the state, although in the case of Pakistan and Iran other sources of law are also recognized. The position of the Islamic clergy is recognized publicly by their level of scholarship coupled with their reputation for personal virtue, not by ordination by a hierarchy. Even in Saudi Arabia and Pakistan, the national political leaders have no particular claim to be scholars of Islam or to speak for the Muslim community. Iran is the only country that can claim their expert jurisprudent or *faqih* to be an authority on Islam who can speak for Iranian Muslims.

Since the national leaders of Muslim countries are not trained to be or recognized as Muslim scholars, where is expertise in Islam to be found? The answer is the same in the twenty-first century as it has been since the tenth century—in the universities and higher schools which specialize in Islamic law and religion. Universities in Nishapur, Cordova, Tunis, Fez, Mecca, Medina, Cairo, Isfahan, Delhi, and many other cities have international reputations that have waxed and waned over the past millennia. The best-known Islamic university throughout this time has been al-Azhar University in Cairo. Its head, the Sheikh al-Azhar, is widely recognized as a major authority on Islam. This does not mean, however, that his statements on any question are accepted by Muslims worldwide.

Islamic judgments are derived from a process of legal reasoning based on a body of Islamic law. In the absence of a prophet,[2] the focus of Islam is the Qur'an (Muslim scripture composed of 114 revelations transmitted to the Prophet Muhammad by the angel Gabriel) and the tradition of Islamic law that is derived from the Qur'an and the community of the Prophet.

Islam means submission to a higher authority, God, who rules over all aspects of human lives. Technically, in classical Islam, since all of life falls under the purview of Islam, Muslims should be governed by Islamic law. In reality, over the centuries, spheres of interest have evolved that recognize many Muslim political and religious leaders and recognize that there are areas of vital concern to the Islamic community for which the views of Islamic scholars should be sought and respected. Other areas are considered separate and can be adjudicated in national, not Islamic, courts or government offices. As Iran has demonstrated, the extent to which any group of Muslims accepts separate spheres for religious and political matters is fluid.

Muslim positions on important social issues have been derived from legal principles formulated during the formative periods of Islam. They follow a framework of legal thinking that allows for different applications as needs arise and puts heavy responsibility on individuals to determine their actions. Family planning is of particular concern because it is a political issue of interest to governments, technocrats, economists, and development planners. Family planning also interests individual Muslims because it affects the community and families. Since these interests often conflict, it is important to understand the view of Muslim scholars who command knowledge of the Qur'an and other sources of law.

This chapter discusses Islamic legal theory on family planning, but there is no intention to discuss the practice of family planning or to imply that all Muslims follow the legal stance laid out below. Nor does this chapter discuss whether religion dictates practice. Data suggest that behavior falls within a context, and Islam is a major part of the context of Muslim behavior, whether the Muslim in question lives in the Middle East, South Asia, Africa, or North America. The impact of Islam in different areas may be tempered by circumstances, including politics, and by the leadership of the 'ulama.

This chapter also emphasizes that Islam, whether the legal tradition, the pronouncements of the 'ulama, or the practice of the individual Muslim, is highly concerned with matters that have an impact upon family and community. Although all Muslims will not respond in a like manner, Islam informs the behavior of many.

Traditional practice enforced by peer pressure in a community is often a more decisive influence than religious pronouncements by Muslim authorities. Such pressure is found in matters of family and gender relations. Individual Muslims may declare many of these matters to be religious questions, sanctioned by Islam, yet religious leaders present divergent positions that differ from those held by individual Muslims in their communities and by other religious leaders.

Definition of Family Planning and Islamic Law

The discussion of family planning in Islam is predicated upon certain points that need to be explicitly set out. First, neither marriage nor progeny is required in Islam, but these are of great importance for stabilizing community mores, organizing a family structure, and averting the social chaos that could result from unregulated sexual contact.

Second, family planning is the process of the husband and wife mutually determining the number and spacing of their children's births to promote the health of the mother and the children and to contribute to the social and economic well-being of the family. Various birth-control methods and contraception contribute to these ends. Also included in family planning is a means to control fertility. The terms "family planning" and, in particular, "contraception" have been invested with the negative sense of seeking to prevent progeny. In an extreme case, this means to prevent all progeny and to thwart the development and well-being of a particular community, here the Muslim community.

Third, Islam has no central authority to speak for or to all Muslims. It is impossible for any one authority to present an opinion binding upon all Muslims. The dispersal of Islam across all major continents and the conversion of disparate cultures have resulted in different interpretations and local standards for Islamic practices. Many consider the system of Islamic law to be the major factor in conserving a strong sense of identity and unity.

Fourth, Islam recognizes no divisions between aspects of a believer's life, such as in the Christian doctrine of the two swords: religious and secular. All areas are encompassed by the revelation of God to Muhammad (the Qur'an) and are equally governed by the law of Islam. Since Islam means submission to the will of God, a Muslim is, therefore, one who places the will of God above his or her own wishes and follows what God commands. The work of Islamic law is to make the religious commandments clear to the believer.

Islamic law includes the law governing rituals of personal religious observance: ritual worship, personal status or civil law, contract law, the law of warfare and booty, social matters (interrelations of the community), and the appointment and expectations of political leadership. The technical term for Islamic law is *shari'a*, the right path to follow.

Sources of Islamic Law

Since the early days of the Muslim community (c. 735 C.E.), Muslims have recognized the importance of determining an established process for setting law. Certain procedures are integral to determining legality. A hierarchy of sources and procedures is applied to questions of practice.

First, the decisive source of law is the Qur'an. A clear textual reference in the Qur'an outweighs all other sources, is considered to be literally the word of God, and is infallible. Second, the source of law next in importance is a written record (hadith) of the words or practice of the Prophet Muhammad or, secondarily, of reputable companions of Muhammad (Sunna). These records are relayed by a chain of authorities. The veracity of these records (many of which scholars consider to be fraudulent, fabricated for various purposes in the first centuries of Islam) is closely tied to the plausibility of the chain of authorities rather than the content of the record. Early Muslim scholars assembled collections of hadith sayings and judged them to be strongly probable or doubtful.

The reasoning behind this source of law stipulates that Muhammad, as the prophet of God, lived as honorable a life as is humanly possible and so should be emulated. This reasoning extends to his companions and assumes that if they were flouting the law or intent of the law, Muhammad would have corrected them. These records also include sayings and actions of Muhammad's family—in particular Ali, his son-in-law (the first Shi'i Imam); Fatima, his daughter; the sons of Ali and Fatima, Hassan and Hussein—and of the first caliphs of Islam: Abu Bakr, Omar, and Othman, although their credibility is less than that of Muhammad.

Third, the next source is the consensus of the Muslim community. Muhammad said in a hadith that his community would never agree in an error. The consensus of the Muslims, and in particular, the consensus of the 'ulama, is regarded as authoritative. This principle of seeking consensus promotes conformity, smoothes divisiveness, and promotes agreement.

Fourth, analogical reasoning seeks precedents in the jurisprudence texts (Qur'anic verses and hadith texts) and reasons from that point. It narrows options and keeps legal conclusions within a circumscribed area. Early in the development of Islamic jurisprudence, independent reasoning or personal opinion was espoused as a source of law by one school of thought. However, mainstream jurists worried that the use of independent reasoning without recourse to precedent would imperil the structure of revelation and legal principles, and the jurists worked to discredit further use.

A principle derived from independent reasoning, *ijtihad* is important in legal reasoning. Ijtihad is the application of reason to the process of legal reasoning that results in a more flexible system while still remaining within the framework of Islamic jurisprudence. In the past century, this principle has been of great interest to Muslims seeking to rework, revive, and apply Muslim principles to contemporary issues without departing from Islamic permissibility. Because of the history of the development of Shi'a Islam, ijtihad has been more used by Shi'a than by Sunni Muslims.

A principle of Islamic law, *istihsan* (seeking the most equitable solution), more prominent in the earlier development of the legal schools, has a possible application. Istihsan, and its counterpart, *istislah* (seeking the best solution for the general interest), were two principles applied when strict analogical reasoning was believed to generate an injustice. Reasoning from the two bases of equity and the public interest was as important in generating a legal opinion as the other, more prominent sources of law. Use of istihsan and istislah diminished over time as they were linked with independent human reason and discredited as human reason was increasingly seen as an unsuitable principle for legal reasoning.

However, istihsan and istislah remain as vitally important guiding principles and as the general purpose of Islamic law.

Categories of Religious Permissibility

Muslims are commanded to ordain the good and forbid the evil. To this end, they need to differentiate between actions that are religiously permissible and those that are prohibited. Islamic law seeks through application of the hierarchy of the sources of law to determine whether an action is obligatory, prohibited, or ranked somewhere in the middle. There are five categories:

a. obligatory—a required action. If the action is not performed, the omission is blameworthy (e.g., the five pillars: the creed, five daily prayers, paying tithes, fasting Ramadan, performing the pilgrimage to Mecca if financially able).

b. recommended—any commendable action but not required. This action is rewarded when performed but when omitted brings no penalty (e.g., marriage and children).

c. indifferent—a neutral action whose performance or omission is neither rewarded nor punished.

d. disapproved—actions that are disapproved but are not punished or forbidden. There are various rankings within this category and a wide divergence of opinion as to what is blameworthy (e.g., divorce or 'azl without the permission of the woman).

e. forbidden—actions whose commission brings punishment (e.g., adultery, stealing, murder).

Schools of Islam

SUNNI ISLAM

In Sunni Islam, four different schools of Islamic jurisprudence have survived and are recognized today. Other schools, prominent during their founder's lifetimes, did not stand the test of time. The four schools include Hanafi (dominant in Central and Western Asia—from Turkey to Afghanistan; Cairo and the Delta in Northern Egypt; Pakistan; and India), Maliki (North Africa, Upper Egypt), Shafi'i (Malaysia, southern Arabia, East Africa, Lower Egypt, South Africa), and Hanbali (Saudi Arabia).

Although remarkably similar in the bulk of their tenets, they differ in their reliance upon particular methods of legal reasoning. For example, the Hanafi School tends to rely more than the others upon independent reasoning. The Maliki School emphasizes use of hadith and the example or living tradition (Sunna) of the Prophet Muhammad. The Shafi'i School developed the major principles of Islamic jurisprudence, adding to the prestige of the hadith texts and the use of analogy. The Hanbali School tends to be rather conservative in reliance on Qur'anic and hadith texts.

These four schools regard each other as fully orthodox, respect each other's positions, and, in practice, have no fundamental differences. One can find examples of jurists of one school differing with the reasoning of their colleagues and taking the position of another school.

SHI'I LEGAL SCHOOLS

The major Shi'ite law school is the Ja'fari (Imami or Twelver), although there are also schools representing the minority Zaydis and Isma'ilis.

Shi'i schools differ from Sunni schools in two major ways, although basic methods of legal reasoning are similar. In particular, their dependence on the authority of their Imams has led them to downplay consensus. The doctrine of the Imam, seen as infallible and divinely guided, places greater reliance upon the Imam's authority. This has led them to greater reliance upon ijtihad than was customary among the Sunnis, for once the Imams were no longer there to guide the community (the twelfth Imam went in occultation in 874 C.E.), scholars were left to interpret the legal texts.

Also, although hadith and Sunna figure prominently in their jurisprudence, the hadith texts diverge from those of the Sunnis and emphasize Muhammad's family and the Imams. In most areas, however, the Sunni and Shi'i law is similar. Strong differences are found in personal status law, primarily the doctrine of temporary marriage.

On family planning (use of 'azl or coitus interruptus), both Sunni and Shi'i schools have much in common. All schools are basically agreed that 'azl is permissible when used with the consent of the wife. Details differ among the schools.

Islamic Legal Positions on Family Planning

LEGAL REASONING IN PRACTICE

Using four different examples—infanticide, 'azl, abortion, and sterilization—this section shows how opinions among jurists developed in the classical Islamic jurisprudence texts, how these techniques apply to contemporary questions of religious permissibility, and where room for differences exists.

FEMALE INFANTICIDE

A pre-Islamic practice of exposing unwanted female children to the elements (*wa'd*) was decisively outlawed by the Qur'an. The relevant passage reads, "when the buried infant shall be asked for what sin she was slain" (81:9). Since there could be no blameless answer to this question, the text is considered a clear prohibition of the practice. No legal discussion is necessary since the Qur'an makes a definitive ruling.

'AZL

The only type of contraception mentioned in the jurisprudence texts is 'azl, the Arabic term for contraception by withdrawal before ejaculation or coitus interruptus. Medical texts mention a variety of other methods, but since religious scholars do not refer to these methods, the legal discussion is limited to 'azl. Jurists from the four major Sunni schools follow the hadith that indicate 'azl was allowed: "We (the companions of the Prophet) used 'azl during the time of the Prophet while the Qur'an was being revealed" (Jabir Ibn Abdullah). A similar version states: "We used to practice 'azl during the time of the Prophet. The Prophet came to know about it, but did not forbid us" (Muslim). A reporter of the tradition (Sufiyan) adds, "Had this been something to be prohibited, the Qur'an would have prohibited us (doing it)."

Other hadith texts are ambiguous but do not negate the permissibility of 'azl as the following samples of frequently cited hadith show. "'I have a slave girl and we need her as a servant and around the palm groves. I have sexual relations with her, but I am afraid of her becoming pregnant.' The Prophet said, 'Practice 'azl with her if you wish, although she will receive what has been predestined for her anyway'" (Jabir). "We rode out with the Prophet of God to raid the Banu Mustaliq and we captured some female prisoners. . . . We desired women and abstinence became hard. We wanted to use 'azl and asked the prophet about that and he said, 'It is all right for you to do so, for God, the Exalted, has predestined what is to be created until Judgment Day" (Abu Said). "The Jews said that 'azl is the small wa'd (infanticide). The Prophet said 'The Jews mislead for if God wanted to create something, no one could avert it'" (Abu Said).

This emphasis upon predestination does not mean that 'azl is forbidden. Rather it shows a strong and contradictory belief in fatalism. This reasoning produces a logical fallacy, for if God has predestined all, whatever one does cannot alter the outcome. Whether one uses 'azl or not is irrelevant since a child will result if it is God's will. Therefore, the individual who uses contraception, attempting to interfere with God's will, shows a lack of faith.

Hadith texts that forbid 'azl liken it to wa'd: "I was present

when the Prophet was in company, saying: 'I was about to prohibit the *ghayla* (becoming pregnant while still nursing a previous
child), but I observed the Byzantines and the Persians and saw
them do it and no harm befell their children.' They then asked him
about *'azl* and the Prophet answered, 'It is hidden infanticide.'"

Given contradictory hadith, the jurists have two choices.
They may inspect the chain of authority of a given text. If it is
problematic, then the hadith is discarded. If it is credible, then the
hadith is evaluated in context with other hadith. Given a variety
of hadith speaking for a given practice, a solitary one speaking
against would generally be disregarded. However, law schools
can emphasize the interpretation they wish, citing hadith texts
and substantiating them with their own interpretation of law and
practice.

In medieval times, the Zahiriya legal school of Ibn Hazm
taught that 'azl was forbidden, using infanticide as a parallel. All
other schools hold that 'azl is permissible; most of them qualify
this by requiring the permission of the wife, if she is a free woman.
Individual scholars or jurists may differ.

Although the act is deemed permissible by the majority of the
hadith texts, most jurists labeled it a blameworthy action. The
noted Shafi'i jurist, al-Ghazzali, labeled 'azl as permitted, reasoning that use of 'azl is analogous to abstention from a preferred
action. While not recommended, it is still lawful.

Theoretically, the wife can request 'azl, but she would have to
have her husband's consent as it is considered to be a contract
between the two.[3] This method of birth control is one controlled
by the husband. Since the writers of the jurisprudence texts were
male, it is natural that they would speak of birth-control measures
of which they personally had knowledge. Medical texts document other methods to prevent pregnancy through infusions,
suppositories, and other means (Himes 1970, 135–69). The jurisprudence texts are silent on female methods of birth control.

POSITIONS OF THE LEGAL SCHOOLS ON 'AZL

Hanafi: 'azl is permitted. Some jurists require the permission of the wife; some state that permission is not necessary when wartime or other difficulties allow exceptional measures.

Maliki: 'azl is permitted if the wife gives her consent. She may be compensated for her consent—paid off, if she so wills.

Shafi'i: 'azl is permitted absolutely, with or without the wife's consent. For some (not including al-Ghazzali), the practice is considered blameworthy. A few jurists require the wife's consent. A few others do not permit it.

Hanbali: 'azl is permitted with the wife's consent. Some jurists believe that consent is not necessary in some conditions, such as when waging war in enemy territory.

Ja'fari (Imami): 'azl is permissible with the wife's consent. Jurists add a caveat that this permission can be given once, at the time of marriage, and is good for all time—even if the wife changes her mind. Like the Maliki School, a few jurists believe the wife's consent is very important, even to the point of giving her monetary compensation if the husband uses 'azl against her will. The fine of ten dinars was seen as a prohibitive sum for recurrent payment (Omran 1988, 292).

Zaydi: 'azl is permissible; jurists differ as to whether the wife's consent is necessary. These views are close to the Shafi'i views.

Isma'ili: Like the Ja'fari school, 'azl is permitted with the wife's consent, but consent can be obtained at the time of the marriage contract.

ABORTION

Islam, like Judaism and Christianity, prohibits taking a human life. The basic question on abortion thereby revolves around when a fetus becomes a person, or when the soul enters the fetus.

Muslim jurists and scholars hold two views on abortion. The first states that abortion is forbidden absolutely (Maliki School). The second follows Qur'anic reasoning that the fetus becomes a human being after 120 days. At this time the soul enters the fetus, and abortion at this point is forbidden. This position takes as its text Qur'anic passages (two are most used) that describe the creation of man:

> O mankind. If you are in doubt as to the Resurrection, [consider] that we have created you of earth; then of semen; then of a blood clot; then of a lump of flesh, formed or not formed, so that we may demonstrate to you [our power] and we establish in the wombs what we will, till a stated term then we bring you out as infants ... (22:4)
>
> We created man of a quintessence of clay. Then we placed him as semen in a firm receptacle. Then we formed the semen in to a blood clot; then we formed the clot into a lump of flesh; then we formed out of that lump bones and clothed the bones with flesh; then we made him another creation. So blessed be God the best Creator. (23:12–4)

The three stages listed beyond the earth or clay stage—semen, blood clot, lump of flesh—were each assigned a 40-day duration by a hadith text: "The Prophet said: Each of you is constituted in your mother's womb for forty days as semen, then it becomes a blood-clot for an equal period, then a lump of flesh for another equal period, then the angel is sent, and he breathes the soul into it."

Adding the first three 40-day stages together, jurists figured that the fetus existed in the womb for 120 days before the soul enters. Following this reasoning, the majority of jurists held that aborting the fetus would be permitted before 120 days elapsed but forbidden as killing the soul after this point. Hanafi jurists permitted abortion until the end of the fourth month. Some jurists, a small minority, held that the fetus can only be aborted during the first 40-day period. The Maliki School prohibited abortion absolutely (Musallim 1974, 57).

Abortion for the health of the mother is generally permissible. Some hold that a compelling reason, such as a threat to the mother's life, harm to a nursing child, or a deformed fetus, can extend permission beyond 120 days (Omran 1984, 332).

The Hanafis permit abortion until after 120 days; many permit it after the end of the fourth month. Some require an excuse; some do not. The majority of Malikis prohibit abortion absolutely. A small minority permits abortion before 40 days. Most Shafi'is agree that abortion is permissible if there is an excuse. Some held to the 40-day limit, some set limits of 80 or 120 days. Most Hanbalis agree with the Hanafis. Like the Shafi'is, various limits for abortion are set: 40, 80, and 120 days. Some Hanbalis prohibit abortion. The Ja'fari Shi'a basically prohibit abortion. Zaydi Shi'a permit abortion without an excuse.

STERILIZATION

There are no legal texts on sterilization, probably because the medical procedures were not current at that time. Sterilization, or the permanent loss of fertility, is not permissible primarily because it permanently alters that which God has created.

All schools prohibit permanent sterilization. Many jurists equate sterilization with castration, which is prohibited. Some classical jurists considered sterilization as a crime that is punishable by law and likened to a murder that requires blood money to be paid (al-Khayyir 1970, 359). The Imami school of law indicated a change in the mid–1980s when Ayatollah Khomeini issued a *fatwa* (formal legal opinion) in favor of sterilization and a later one in favor of vasectomy (Carol Underwood, personal communication, 19 September 2003). In most countries this prohibition of permanent sterilization is circumvented by physicians who maintain that tubal ligations and vasectomies may be reversed and are thereby nonpermanent and legal.

Applications of Islamic Law to Family Planning

Classical Islamic legal reasoning is followed by contemporary 'ulama. To show a person's background in Islamic law and religion, various titles are used. A *mufti* (usually only one, if at all, in a given country) is considered a legal or religious expert. He can issue a fatwa that takes legal precedent thoroughly into account. Certain positions, such as Sheikh al-Azhar, the head of the traditional Islamic college (now a modern university) in Cairo, tend to carry weight across national boundaries.

In Iran, religious scholars form a hierarchy. Each is considered a *mujtahid* and exercises ijtihad, but occupies a different rank in the hierarchy, the highest now being that of faqih, which is modeled after the slot the Ayatollah Khomeini held as the final point of review for Islamic law. Sunni Muslims may be given the title Sheikh or Imam, which denotes respect. This use of the term "imam" is fundamentally different from the Shi'i use. For Sunni Muslims, the imam leads a congregation in prayer. It does not denote high education or expertise in Islamic studies. For Shi'a Muslims, Imam refers to Ali and his descendents, who succeeded Muhammad as spokesmen for the Muslim community.

A question considered by the 'ulama is how Islam applies the technological advances of the twentieth century and judges the permissibility or prohibition of practices unknown during the formative period of Islamic law, for example, contraception. Since rising birth rates have threatened economic growth in Muslim countries, numerous 'ulama have made pronouncements on the religious permissibility of family planning. Most agree that Islam permits use of contraception (pills, IUDs, prophylactics, diaphragms, foam).

The majority of scholars who permit the use of family planning reason from the medieval jurisprudence texts. By using analogical reasoning they argue that family-planning use is permitted as long as the husband and wife are mutually agreed. This argument refers to the position of jurists on 'azl. As contemporary methods of family planning parallel 'azl in preventing the union of sperm and egg, they should be judged on the same basis.

One major difference is that men control the use of 'azl, which requires the woman's permission for its use (in the majority of the legal texts). Since women control the use of pills, IUDs, and so forth, likewise the man should give his permission. Scholars offer a solution by calling for the joint permission of the spouses for any method of family planning.

Most 'ulama worldwide support the husband's and wife's right of family-planning measures to determine the number and spacing of their children. Their positions are solidly supported by Islamic jurisprudence. Opposition to family planning among the ranks of 'ulama relates more to demographic and political realities than to theological arguments, although references to theological concerns are made.

A primary division exists between the nations experiencing a demographic crunch (e.g., Iran, Egypt, Tunisia, Morocco) and those that seek to increase their population (e.g., Iraq, Saudi Arabia, Kuwait, Libya). 'Ulama from the first group are more likely to espouse a pro-family-planning position than are 'ulama from the second group.

For the past twenty years, Western nations, Western technocrats, and Western-dominated multilateral agencies have called for a lower birthrate in the lesser-developed world. Many Muslims and 'ulama feel that their religious community is being targeted to restrict population and to limit power and influence. A proponent of this position is the late Mawlana Mawdoudi of Pakistan.

Opponents to family planning employ arguments that are based on strands of thought in the Qur'an or hadith. These arguments reflect the importance of children to the immediate family for whom they are the joy of life (many hadith support this) and the importance of numerous progeny to produce a strong Islamic community, the argument of quantity or multitude of Muslims.

Qur'anic verses that refer to procreation, children, and offspring are quoted:

> And Allah has made for you mates from yourselves and made for you out of them children and grandchildren. (16:72)

> And verily we sent messengers before you and we gave them wives and offspring. (13:38)

> And remember, when you were but few, how did He help you multiply. (7:86)

> And who say: Our Lord! Vouchsafe us comfort of our wives and our offspring (make them the joy and the apple of our eyes). (25:74)

An important hadith text which is much quoted and recorded in various versions is:

> Marry and multiply, for I shall make a display of you before other nations of the Day of Judgment.

A numerous community has traditionally been seen as strong, militarily potent, and able to provide economically for its members. A small population was associated with weakness and the inability to represent its own efforts.

A former Sheikh al-Azhar, Muhammad Shaltut (appointed by Jamal Abd al-Nasser in the 1960s), spoke directly to this point and sought to negate it. He made the argument that populations (Egypt as a case in point) were growing so rapidly that additional numbers would not strengthen the community as a whole, but weaken it. He stated that in order to be strong and influential, Muslims had to emphasize quality rather than quantity; that is, limit their population size and work at educating their population. Proponents of unrestricted population growth were ignoring the real problems: disease, underdevelopment, and illiteracy.

Theologians and less-educated religious leaders in the countryside bring up predestination. The Qur'an states:

"Kill not your children, on a plea of want, we provide sustenance for you and for them." (6:151). [This verse is also a condemnation of infanticide.]

There is not a creature on earth, but its sustenance depends on Allah. He knows its habitation and its depository. All is in a clear record. (11:6)

(They prayed): Our Allah! On you we rely, and to you we turn in repentance, and to you is our final journey.
     And he who fears Allah, He will find a way out for him, and He will provide for him from whence he has no expectation, and whosoever relies on Allah, sufficient is Allah for him. Lo! Allah brings his command to pass. Allah has set a measure for all things. (65: 2–3)

The principle of sustenance, or God providing, along with reliance upon God is seen as a basic argument against worrying about resources to support a family. A fatalistic view, that all is ordained by God and will follow through as He wills, supports this view. Belief in predestination is a highly simplified adaptation of a complex theological argument that raged in Islamic intellectual circles for centuries. The synthesis of a strong belief in free will by one school and a fatalistic, determinist view of another school was advocated by the Ashariya, which became the dominant theological school in Sunni Islam. Al-Ashari and, after him, al-Ghazzali did not argue for predestination, but rather a subtle compromise between the two positions whereby God's will was supreme, but humans nevertheless were responsible for their own actions. Over time, the subtleties were mostly lost, and belief in predestination became common among the less well-educated.

Another argument against birth control that generally is not explicitly stated is that use of contraception may free women from their traditional roles as wives and mothers.

Major arguments for family planning by contemporary theologians include the importance of nursing children well to inoculate them against disease and to ensure adequate nutrition to cut down on infant mortality figures. The Qur'an enjoins women to nurse for two years. The Arabs have a term, *ghayla*, which means becoming pregnant while nursing a child. The loss of nutrients in the breast milk that go to the fetus is seen as condemning the nursing child to ill health and weakness that could result in death.

On the authority of Asma' bint Zayd Ibn al-Sakan who said: "I heard the Prophet say: 'Do not kill your children unconsciously. For al-ghayla will have [in the future] the same effect as when a horseman is overtaken [by an opponent] and thrown off his horse.'" (Abu Daoud)

Many Muslim jurists consider nursing a newborn child to be a method of family planning and proclaim its use for that purpose, saying that Islam has recognized the need for family planning and provided nursing as a means. This is disinformation for women who then believe that nursing will prevent pregnancy.

Another argument is the need to space children, not only to prevent ghayla, but also to preserve the woman's health. Many jurists consider preservation of her beauty a sufficient point.

Many religious scholars and religious leaders who support the Islamic permissibility of family planning may not support the dissemination of family-planning information by national governments. The reason is that any program advocated by the government could be understood by the populace as mandatory. For them, it is vital that family planning remain a decision taken in the realm of the family, not one imposed by the state.

ABORTION AND STERILIZATION

Abortion is illegal in every Muslim country except Tunisia and Turkey (where it is limited), which shows the unpopularity of the practice. Contemporary 'ulama are divided on the religious permissibility of abortion; some permit abortion in the first four months and some prohibit it absolutely. Most 'ulama, however, note that when the mother's health is endangered, the question becomes a medical rather than a religious one, and the doctor's recommendation becomes the final word.

Permanent sterilization is prohibited, although exceptions are listed for families with genetic disease. Temporary sterilization, by analogy to 'azl, is permitted by some 'ulama.

FUNDAMENTALIST ISLAM AND FAMILY PLANNING

Various terms—fundamentalism, resurgence, revivalism, militant, political, Islamism, Muslim activism—have been used to describe an increasing political activism in the name of Islam by various Muslim groups. Some groups are affiliated with governments; some operate in opposition. The groups have similar views but rarely operate in concert. Activist Islam designates a politicized, mobilized form of Islam that uses Islamic symbolism and legitimation for political action. While activist theologians work out applications of Islamic principles in line with their views, the thrust of their teachings is primarily directed at political organization and mobilization.

Examples of the scope of activist groups include supporters of the Ayatollah Khomeini who control Iran's government; the Shi'i Movement of the Deprived led by Musa Sadr in Lebanon that spawned both the secular Amal and the radically religious Hezbollah; Pakistan's Jamaat-e-Islami; Islamic political parties, such as the Malaysian Islamic Party, Turkey's Refah and AK parties, the Algerian Islamic Salvation Front, and the Jordanian Islamist blocs, which have won significant votes in national elections; the Muslim Youth Movement of Malaysia; the radical Muslim groups

Takfir wal-Hegira, the Islamic Association and the like (in Egypt); the Syrian, Jordanian, and Egyptian Muslim Brotherhoods; and Hamas, the Palestinian Muslim Brotherhood. Although their names are similar, the Muslim Brotherhoods' policies differ. The Syrian Muslim Brotherhood was virtually wiped out by the Syrian army in 1982; the Muslim Brotherhood in Egypt is the moderate granddaddy of all the activist groups. Hamas has become more tied to violence through support for suicide bombing. In addition, governments with strong ties to Islam such as that of Saudi Arabia could be seen (by some observers and at various periods) as fundamentalist.

Although religious in orientation, Islamic activists state their issues in sociopolitical language. These issues include the system utilized by national governments; the law that rules the country, secular or Islamic; the nature of distributive justice and the search for social and economic equity; participation in the political system; income cleavage and class systems; and the question of identity in a changing world. These questions relate to the process of social change taking place in their societies. They see the West as a great threat to their political autonomy and to their religious values.

Despite the differences among the various groups, there are important similarities. The lack of distinction between religion and state is generally accepted in Islam; these groups emphasize this point and call for a return to Islamic law in place of systems derived from Western law. Religious symbolism is increasingly important in political questions. While national leaders have always been careful—whatever their politics—of the need to respect Muslim sensibilities, the situation has become more acute. Activists reject programs by labeling them atheistic or imported; in other words, nonauthentic or un-Islamic. Consequentially, governments have been pressured to ban practices seen as un-Islamic and to place emphasis upon Islamic values in educational curricula.

The questions of family planning are of great import to most activist groups. Other concerns are the reworking of gender roles, the relationships of family members, and the confrontation of Western social mores with established tradition. Surveys of reforms in personal status codes throughout the Muslim world demonstrate concerted resistance to change by parties that are generally far more open to analogous change on a political or economic level. Questions on women and family strike a chord of resistance far deeper than other political reforms.

Muslim activists generally attack the concept of family planning and, in particular, government attempts to establish national family-planning programs. They muster arguments based on the need for a strong and numerous Muslim community, the necessity to rely upon God for one's sustenance, and the ability to command resources in a more productive fashion; they accuse the West of seeking to limit Muslim populations by using methods reminiscent of genocide.

In a moderate journal published by the Egyptian Muslim Brotherhood, *al-Da'wa*, the Sheikh al-Azhar in 1977 wrote an essay entitled "Birth Control is a Refuted Idea." His arguments followed the line that birth control is not needed and is basically un-Islamic.

> God is capable of providing food to every human being on earth. The idea of Egypt's limited resources is also a myth. Egyptian deserts are vast and contain plentiful resources. The deserts can be cultivated, and some plants like olive trees endure lack of water for three years. What are needed are dedicated and daring people to conquer the desert and use its resources. Indeed Egypt may suffer a manpower shortage in the future. (Dessouki 1982, 20)

A 1979 article made the point that use of birth control leads to the spread of immorality due to increased use of abortion and premarital sex or adultery. During 1980 and 1981, in response to the Egyptian government's mass media program emphasizing the use of family planning, almost every issue of this magazine had at least one reference to birth control (Dessouki 1982, 20). These arguments do not only appeal to fundamentalists but are common throughout sectors of the Middle East and North Africa. In Morocco, for example, similar arguments are often heard and have significant popular support.

University students represent much of the strength of the fundamentalist/activist movements. Student surveys designed to measure sympathies with activist beliefs focus on relations between men and women and the establishment of Islamic law as the sole law of the state. In a sample of four hundred Moroccan students interviewed in 1984, 11 percent believed men and women should not mix in public places; 32 percent favored the reestablishment of Islamic law as the sole law of the state (Munson 1986, 274).

A 1984 survey of Egyptian medical students demonstrated strong differences between male and female responses concerning family planning. Twenty-six percent of the male respondents stated that they believed family planning was contrary to the beliefs of Islam, 9 percent of the female students responded similarly, and 15 percent of the male students refused to answer.

Open-ended questioning solicited negative reasoning from the respondents in line with the arguments of the activists. One medical student defined family planning as "taking care of the members of the family and not limiting birth because this is God's job." Another stated, "This is only God's affair, and if there is social justice and application of Islamic laws, there would be no need to restrict birth." Another commented, "Unfortunately family planning is a bad theory applied, fortunately with bad organization, so it is not doing any harm" (al-Mehairy 1984, 132).

Even governments with firm activist credentials can be put in the awkward position of having to disallow firmly held tenets of belief as to family planning because of exigencies of national development. The most recent case, Iran, pursued a strong pro-natalist policy designed to discredit the Shah's policy of personal status legal reform and to repopulate the country following the eight-year war with Iraq. In the mid-1990s, because of a booming birth rate, Iranian citizens were advised to limit family size; some citizens believe that no more than two children should be allowed. At the same time, the government's firm stand prohibiting abortion has been eased, but there has been no formal policy change.

Education Level and Religious Arguments on Family Planning

As stated above, 'ulama are the top level of a hierarchy of men, along with a few women, trained in Islamic religious science and Arabic language. They are professors of history, religious language, and law at universities, and they may be employed as ministry officials or judges. Some may be professional writers, doctors, or engineers. Religious leaders on a local level serve as prayer leaders (imam) of mosques and instructors in Qur'anic schools, teaching kindergarten children the essentials of religion and the alphabet.

Depending upon their rank, religious leaders have received very different religious educations. Other key factors include the status of the school attended and the ability of the student himself or herself. The training of religious leaders in rural areas is generally inferior to that in larger towns or cities. Leaders rank by educational training from the top 'ulama, to imams in cities or larger towns, to village imams or Qur'anic schoolteachers.

In Arabic (and generally in each Arabic dialect) the terms are distinct; 'ulama is a technical term and would not be applied to any but the best-trained and most-respected scholars. They, correspondingly, have the highest status. Village-level religious leaders would be called imams, faqih (plural *fuqaha*), or *taleb* (plural *tolba*).

In Shi'ite Islam, terminology differentiates between ranks of religious leaders to a greater extent than in Sunni nations. The lowest level of religious leaders, those in poor city quarters and rural villages, are referred to as *mullahs* (or *akhund*, a more derogatory term); *mujtahids* are differentiated by ranking that acknowledges the degree of the person's training, body of work produced, and respect of citizens and other scholars. The highest general ranking is *ayatollah*. Grand *ayatollah*, or *Marja-i Taqlid*, designates ayatollahs with superior skills.

Classical jurisprudence texts provide the Islamic position on family planning for the medieval period and demonstrate the legal reasoning of scholars. The 'ulama speak authoritatively on adapting those texts to modern problems. But local religious leaders may be the primary voice of Islam for inhabitants of villages and poorer city quarters.

A physician based in an Egyptian rural clinic said:

> The religious leaders here do not approve of family planning and, since the rural areas are geared more to the religious leaders' opinions and pronunciations, it is very difficult to convince the people. One word from the local Sheik equals ten words from me and, therefore, I am in a weak position trying to make them understand the concept of family planning, since the religious leaders themselves are not convinced. (Warwick 1982, 156)

We have few data on the understanding of this stratum of religious leaders across the Middle East. Data from Morocco suggest that local religious leaders espouse a highly simplified version of arguments that 'ulama present in full complexity. They also reason from a different departure point.

When questioned as to the position of Islam on family planning, local Moroccan religious leaders without exception replied

that Islam forbids family planning. In substantiation of their position, they cited the hadith text: "Marry, procreate, and multiply
that I may make a display of you on Judgment Day." This was taken
as a divine command not to be countermanded. Like a minority
of the classical jurists, they also argued in favor of predestination,
stating that family planning is contrary to God's will.

> Public opinion is divided about family planning. Some people think
> it is a good idea; some want children to have them work and bring in
> more money to the family. But in Islam, people should marry when
> they have enough money to take care of a family. Islam is against
> family planning. Whatever God ordains for man should not be
> challenged by man's programs.
>
> God is all-powerful; whatever he wills is decisive. There are no
> specific numbers of children given to a family; only whatever God
> grants. It is not right for others to interfere with the will of God.
> Whatever is written is written (*maktub*). By using contraceptives or
> deciding the size of a family, one interferes with God's will. Whether
> others in the Moroccan government say it is a beneficial program
> and is permitted by Islam is unimportant. Even if everyone from
> the King on down said the program was permissible, the program
> still would not be. The teachings of Islam are against it, and God is
> a higher authority.

Local leaders often made the point that God will provide for
his creations (man), and they have no need for recourse to programs that counter Islamic teachings (Bowen 1981, 196–201).
An Egyptian physician summarized much of the problem:

> Some sheiks have said in the Friday sermon that family planning is
> sinful and against the Muslim religion. There are some Imams here
> who advocate family planning, but their words do not carry much
> weight since they have as many as nine children. The people are not
> convinced by them very much (Warwick 1982, 156).

The middle-rank group of men, here called imams, falls between the highly educated 'ulama and the poorly educated village religious leaders. They are generally graduates of an Islamic secondary school or some facility of higher education. Most often they are employed as imams in mosques serving a good-sized congregation and also as instructors for local Qur'anic schools where they teach a broader curriculum than in a village school.

Their responses were varied, some were anti–family planning for reasons of predestination (i.e., God's will); some cited the hadith to marry and procreate. Others felt that family planning endangered the strength of the Muslim community (and the Moroccan nation) by reducing the number of Muslims.

One young imam, fresh out of school, noted the difference between family planning, which he supported, and birth control, which he did not support. Family planning was a good program as it was directed toward teaching and bringing up children well. He basically repeated the same reasoning as the 'ulama.

> Islam says nothing to limit the number of children in a family or on the other hand to specify a number that should be reached. God will provide what is best for the family in the sense of providing for the children as well as in the sense of caring for the family.
>
> Birth control is dangerous since we as mortals are limited in our intelligence. As we can't predict the future we could find ourselves, having utilized contraceptives, inhabiting a world without sufficient population. We can't judge what others are going to do.
>
> If a husband and wife agree to use contraception, then it is all right as a personal family matter. However, birth control should not be set up as a program. The woman's health is also to be taken into consideration. If her health is endangered, then contraception is naturally permitted. Contraception is not forbidden, but undesirable as a program for the whole nation. (field notes, 1973)

A conclusion, therefore, can be drawn between the level of education of religious leaders and the sophistication of their arguments (complexity of analysis, knowledge of texts) on family planning. All of the religious leaders noted that abortion (unless called for by a doctor to protect the health of the mother) and sterilization were prohibited by Islam.

Conclusion

The image of Islam, and particularly of the Islamic religious sciences, has suffered in the West for more than a century from the sense of being a reactionary, tradition-bound force governed by old bearded men with no sense of the needs of the modern world. Islamic law has been seen as an ossified remnant of the medieval ages. The study of contraception as laid out by the Islamic legal sources proves the opposite.

The meshing of the different sources of Islamic law demonstrates a flexibility and an elegance in coming to grips with a sensitive question by using a technical approach that espouses underlying assumptions of Islamic law: the value of marriage and the family, the importance of contracts, the inviolability of life, and the emphasis on the needs and rights of individuals. At the same time the law attempts to reconcile the delicate balance between individual needs and the welfare of the community.

Historically, major religious traditions have emphasized families as a basic component of society, and the majority of religious hierarchies hesitate to retreat from a pro-natality stance. Support for contraception is commonly suspected to be a secularizing trend, a retreat from a faithful position whereby God provides for his creations.

Islam has no hesitation in recognizing the sexual side of man's human nature and, concomitantly, the necessity of channeling sexual drives into marriage to support, rather than undermine, social order. Ulama question the viability of monastic life, stating that depriving man of family and sexual expression is detrimental—and purposeless. Likewise, divorce is viewed in a practical fashion. Although it is labeled the most reprehensible of all acts not expressly forbidden, divorce is a sensible solution to an untenable marriage.

Contraception to avoid pregnancy is not a prominent feature of classical Muslim family law. Rather, it is an exception for which one must have an acceptable reason. In time, this was formalized in the jurisprudence texts. The 'ulama disregarded reasons for contraception (impregnating women captured in warfare or impregnating a slave girl, which would change her status) and instead concentrated on the rights of the female sexual partner that could be violated by use of contraception. Free wives, as opposed to slaves (concubines) or wives who were also slaves, had rights that some legal schools felt were contravened by use of contraception.

The conflict would be resolved if the wife agreed to contraceptive use, thereby forgoing her rights, and the action would be permissible. Essentially a contract was formed: the man extended an offer (the use of contraception, 'azl) and the woman could either accept—thereby forgoing her rights to children and completing the contract—or reject the offer. Only free wives, many schools of law felt, had the right to form the contract. (Opinions are divided on the complicated subject of what rights concubines and slave wives had, but today's scarcity of those two categories has rendered most of this argument moot.)

The brevity of the section on contraception in each jurisprudence text shows that birth control was an exception to established practice and to expectations that children are a vital product of a marriage. Even today, a man's virility and a woman's fertility are prime determining factors in their social status and standing in their communities.

The views of less-educated Muslim religious leaders, which are contrary to the vast majority of Islamic jurisprudence texts, can be attributed to their lack of understanding of the sophisticated legal texts. Lacking sufficient expertise or acquaintance with the texts, the religious leaders of village or city quarters hold to hadith or principles of religion gleaned from other studies. These simpler, less flexible opinions generally do not reflect the depth of knowledge of legal processes of the more educated 'ulama, nor do they utilize the subtlety of argumentation.

Some contemporary 'ulama resist the attempt by technocrats, government officials, and foreign experts to stretch the legal position on contraception into a government-sanctioned policy on family planning. They see family-planning policy as a means to negate the primary purpose of the family—to produce progeny—rather than seeing it as a device for regulation. Part of their opposition is based on suspicion of government motives and enforcement power.

Although Islam theoretically encompasses all areas of life, many Muslims feel that governments and politics have become increasingly unresponsive to their concerns. Activist Muslims oppose standing governments as not representing the interests of Islam. Although Islam in theory includes governance as falling within the sphere of the Muslim community, ironically, in practice the inverse is true. Governments of Muslim countries have at times attempted to utilize Islam to promote their own ends, to legitimate programs, and to unify factions opposed to their control. Family-planning programs have been a case in point as governments seek Islamic legal decisions (fatwas) favorable to their policies.

The principle of intention (niyya) is important in Islamic law. Religious permissibility of an action is not of paramount importance, but the intention with which a believer performs an act is. Thus, an action such as eating pork, which may be prohibited, may become licit during famine. Would one starve to death or consume pork? A good Muslim would be ruled by the intention behind his action—that the consumption of pork preserved life and was therefore licit. This application of the principle of community interest (istihsan) and the importance of integrity as the basis of one's religious duty is integral to Islamic religious practice.

The conflicts between family-planning purposes and Islamic values make for a difficult fit. Family planning, with its emphasis upon the health and economic well-being of the family unit and preservation of the health of the mother, is totally compatible with Islamic values. On the other hand, Muslims oppose family planning for reasons including questions of God's will, support for large families, and political arguments opposing Western meddling in Muslim matters.

Introducing government into the equation also alters its outcome. What is seen as government supported is then suspect, for most Middle Easterners believe that governments are generally not up to much good. Religious leaders oppose government pronouncements because they feel that whatever the government suggests soon becomes mandatory, if not in fact, at least in many citizens' minds.

Nevertheless, for centuries legal reasoning has emphasized that the possibility for contraception is present in Islamic law. The principles underlying this position may ultimately be more significant than the brief mention of 'azl. In their approach to 'azl to prevent pregnancy, the majority of contemporary 'ulama consistently affirmed the principle of individual responsibility. Both spouses have rights: the right not to contract a pregnancy and the right to refuse 'azl. This throws responsibility upon the shoulders of the husband and wife and essentially states that, although family size bears on larger questions of community needs and welfare, the ultimate decision is up to the couple.

However tangled the issues of family planning become in questions of governmental power, religious opposition, and popular beliefs and practices, the basic position of classical and contemporary Islamic law is clear: It affirms the rights of individuals to make their own decisions on questions regarding their family and its composition.

Notes

1. Until the late nineteenth century, all education in Muslim lands revolved around the religious sciences. Consequently, all educated persons were expert in areas of Islamic religion, law, or Arabic language. While many scholars taught in the universities, others took government positions such as judges, notaries, and bureaucrats. The increasing Western influence in the Muslim world introduced a parallel system of education based on empirical science. The upshot of the parallel system has been the decline of widespread Islamic education above the elementary level. Advanced technical instruction in the Islamic sciences is generally limited to universities, theological colleges, or graduate faculties with an exclusively Islamic curriculum. Iran is an exception.
2. The Qur'an states that Muhammad is the "seal" of the prophets, meaning that he was the last of the prophets of Islam.
3. 'Azl is considered a contract between the husband and wife in that the husband proffers the semen by ejaculating, and the wife accepts the semen. If she does not wish to complete the transaction or the contract, she is not legally obligated to accept the ejaculation.

Bibliography

Adam, Andre. 1975. "Le changement dans le maghreb independant: Acculturation ou reculturation?" *Revue de l'Occident Musulman et de la Mediterranee* 19: 7–15.

Afshar, Haleh. 1982. "Khomeini's teachings and their implications for women." *Feminist Review* 12: 58–72.

Aghajanian, Akbar. 1988. "The value of children in rural and urban Iran: A pilot study." *Journal of Comparative Family Studies* 19: 85–97.

Ahmed, Bashir. 1987. "Determinants of contraceptive use in rural Bangladesh: The demand for children, supply of children, and costs of fertility regulation." *Demography* 24(3): 361–73.

Ahmed, Nilufer R. 1981. "Family size and sex preferences among women in rural Bangladesh." *Studies in Family Planning* 12: 100–9.

Aitken, Annie, and John Stoeckel. 1971. "Dynamics of the Muslim-Hindu Differential in Family Planning Practices in Rural East Pakistan." *Social Biology* 18(3): 268–76.

Ashford, Lori S. 1995. "New Perspectives on Population: Lessons from Cairo." *Population Bulletin* 50: 11–44.

Azari, Farah. 1983. "Sexuality and Women's Oppression in Iran." In *Women of Iran: The Conflict with Fundamental Islam*, edited by Farah Azari, 90–156. London: Ithaca Press.

Badraoui, M. H. H., and O. El-Zeini. 1980. "IUD and Family Planning in Islamic Populations." *Contraceptive Delivery Systems* 1: 325–31.

Bauer, Janet L. 1985. "Sexuality and the Moral 'Construction' of Women in an Islamic Society." *Anthropological Quarterly* 58(3): 120–9.

Bonhomme, J., and A. M. Loubiere. 1971. "La contraception chez les Musulmanes vivant dans la region parisienne." *Revue Francaise de Gynecologie et d'Obstetrique* 66(6): 421–6.

Bonierbale, M., J. Gensollen, and M. Pin. 1981. "La femme immigreé et la sexualité." *Psychologie Medicale* 13(11): 1785–8.

Bouzidi, Mohammed. 1979. "L'Islam et la societe Marocaine face a la contraception." *Annuaire de l'Afrique du Nord* 18: 285–303.

Bowen, Donna Lee. 1980. "Islam and Family Planning in Morocco." *Maghreb Review* 3(10): 20–29.

———. 1981. "Muslim Juridical Opinions Concerning the Status of Women as Demonstrated by the Case of 'Azl." *Journal of Near Eastern Studies* 40(4): 323–28.

———. 1993. "Pragmatic Morality: Islam and Family Planning in Morocco." In *Everyday Life in the Contemporary Middle East*, edited Donna Lee Bowen and E. A. Early, 91–101. Bloomington: Indiana University Press.

———. 1997. "Islam, Abortion, and the 1994 Cairo Population Conference." *International Journal of Middle Eastern Studies* 29(2): 161–84.

Brown, K. L. 1981. "The Campaign to Encourage Family Planning in Tunisia and Some Responses at the Village Level." *Middle Eastern Studies* 17(1): 64–84.

Castineira, Abdul Hasib. 1984. "An Islamic View of the Place of Women." *Arabia* 4(38): 24–5.

Chamratrithirong, Aphichat, Peerasit Kamnuansilpa, and John Knodel. 1986. "Contraceptive Practice and Fertility in Thailand: Results of the Third Contraceptive Prevalence Survey." *Studies in Family Planning* 17(6): 278–87.

Coulson, Noel J. 1969. *Conflicts and Tensions in Islamic Jurisprudence*. Chicago: University of Chicago Press.

Dessouki, Ali E. Hillal, ed. 1982. *Islamic Resurgence in the Arab World*. New York: Praeger.

Dixon, Ruth B. 1976. "The Roles of Rural Women: Female Seclusion, Economic Production, and Reproductive Choice." In *Population and*

Development: The Search for Selective Interventions, edited by Ronald G. Ridker, 290–321. Baltimore: Johns Hopkins University Press.

El-Hamamsy, Laila Shukry. 1974. "Islamic Society and Family Planning: Are They Incompatible?" *Unicef News* 78(Dec.–Jan.): 36–41.

El-Mehairy, Theresa. 1984. "Attitudes of a Group of Egyptian Medical Students Towards Family Planning." *Social Science Medicine* 19(2): 131–4.

El Tom, A. R., D. Lauro, A. A. Farah, R. McNamara, and E. F. Ali Ahmed. 1989. "Family Planning in the Sudan: A Pilot Project Success Story." *World Health Forum* 10: 333–43.

Fakhr El-Islam, M., Taha H. Malasi, and Sanaa I. Abu-Dagga. 1988. "Oral Contraceptives, Sociocultural Beliefs, and Psychiatric Symptoms." *Social Science Medicine* 27(9): 941–5.

Faour, Muhammad. 1989. "Fertility Policy and Family Planning in the Arab Countries." *Studies in Family Planning* 20(5): 254–63.

Farrag, Osama A., Mohammad S. Rahman, Jessica Rahman, Tapan K. Chatterjee, and M. Hisham Al-Sibai. 1983. "Attitude Towards Fertility Control in the Eastern Province of Saudi Arabia." *Saudi Medical Journal* 4(2): 111–6.

Fricke, Thomas E., Sabiha H. Syed, and Peter C. Smith. 1986. "Rural Punjabi Social Organization and Marriage Timing Strategies in Pakistan." *Demography* 23(4): 489–508.

Good, Mary-Jo DelVecchio. 1980. "Of Blood and Babies: The Relationship of Popular Islamic Physiology to Fertility." *Social Science and Medicine* 14B(3): 147–56.

Hafez, E. S. E., ed. 1980. *IUDs and Family Planning: Progress in Contraceptive Delivery Systems*. No. 2. Boston: G.K. Hall Medical Publishers.

Hathout, H. 1972. "Abortion and Islam." *Lebanon Medical Journal* 25(3): 237–9.

Himes, Norman E. 1936, 1970. *Medical History of Contraception*. New York: Schocken Books.

Hoque, Zohurul. 1970. "Religion of Islam on Family Planning." *Family Planning News* (April–May): 3–6.

Inhorn, Marcia C. 1996. *Infertility and Patriarchy: The Cultural Politics of Gender and Family Life in Egypt*. Philadelphia: University of Pennsylvania Press.

International Planned Parenthood Federation, Middle East and North Africa Region. 1974. *Islam and Family Planning*. Beirut: International Planned Parenthood Federation.

Issawi, Charles. 1985. Review of *Sex and Society in Islam: Birth Control before the Nineteenth Century*, by Basim F. Musallam. *Journal of the American Oriental Society* 105(2): 362–3.

al-Kadhi, Ann Bragdon. 1985. "Women's education and its relation to fertility: Report from Baghdad." In *Women and the Family in the Middle East: New Voices of Change*, edited by Elizabeth Warnock Fernea, 145–7. Austin: University of Texas Press.

Khalifa, Mona A. 1988. "Attitudes of Urban Sudanese Men Toward Family Planning." *Studies in Family Planning* 19(4): 236–43.

al-Khayyir, Rahman. 1970. "The Attitude of Islam toward Abortion and Sterilization." In *Islam and Family Planning*, vol. 2, edited by Isam R. Nazar, 345–62. Beirut: International Planned Parenthood Federation.

Khan, M. E., and C. V. S. Prasad. 1980. *Fertility Control in India*. New Delhi: Manohar Publications.

Lerman, Charles, John W. Molyneaux, Soetedjo Moeljodihardjo, and Sahala Pandjaitan. 1989. "The Correlation between Family Planning Program Inputs and Contraceptive Use in Indonesia." *Studies in Family Planning* 20(1): 26–37.

Longworthy, Nancy, and Harry Fierman. 1988. "Family Planning in Egypt: A Planning Response to an Islamic Environment." *International Journal of Health Planning and Management* 3: 127–33.

Mahdavi, Shireen. 1985. "The Position of Women in Shi'a Iran: Views of the 'Ulama." In *Women and the Family in the Middle East: New Voices of Change*, edited by Elizabeth Warnock Fernea, 255–68. Austin: University of Texas Press.

Moghadam, Val. 1988. "Women, Work, and Ideology in the Islamic Republic." *International Journal of Middle East Studies* 20: 221–43.

Mueller, Eric. 1985. "Revitalizing Old Ideas: Developments in Middle Eastern Family Law." In *Women and the Family in the Middle East: New Voices of Change*, edited by Elizabeth Warnock Fernea, 224–8. Austin: University of Texas Press.

Munson, Henry, Jr. 1986. "The Social Base of Islamic Militancy in Morocco." *Middle East Journal* 40(Spring): 267–84.

Musallam, B. F. 1974. "The Islamic Sanction of Contraception." In *Population and its Problems: A Plain Man's Guide*, edited by H. B. Parry, 300–10. Oxford: Clarendon Press.

———. 1981. "Why Islam Permitted Birth Control." *Arab Studies Quarterly* 3(2): 181–97.

————. 1983. *Sex and Society in Islam.* New York: Cambridge University Press.

Nagi, Mostafa H. 1983. "Trends in Moslem Fertility and the Application of the Demographic Transition Model." *Social Biology* 30(3): 245–62.

Nazer, Isam. 1980. "The Tunisian Experience in Legal Abortion." *International Journal of Gynaecology and Obstetrics* 17(5): 488–92.

Obermeyer, Carla M.. 1992. "Islam, Women, and Politics: The Demography of Arab Countries." *Population and Development Review* 18(1): 33–60.

————. 1993. "Culture, Maternal Health Care, and Women's Status: A Comparison of Morocco and Tunisia." *Studies in Family Planning* 24(6): 354–65.

————, ed. 1995. *Family, Gender, and Population in the Middle East: Policies in Context.* Cairo: American University in Cairo Press.

Omran, Abdel Rahim. 1984. *Population Problems and Prospects in the Arab World.* Cairo: United Nations Fund for Population Activities.

————. 1988. *Family Planning in the Legacy of Islam.* Cairo: United Nations Fund for Population Activities.

al-Qasimi, Mujahid ul-Islam. 1978. "Natural Family Planning in Islam." *Jami Notes* (Deoband, Pakistan): 52–3.

Ragab, M. Ismail. 1981. "Islam and the Unwanted Pregnancy." In *Abortion and Sterilization: Medical and Social Aspects*, edited by Jane E. Hodgson, 507–18. New York: Academic Press.

Rosenberg, Michael J., Roger W. Rochat, Suraiya Jabeen, Anthony R. Measham, M. Obaidullah, and Atiqur R. Khan. 1981. "Attitudes of Rural Bangladesh Physicians Toward Abortion." *Studies in Family Planning* 12: 318–21.

Sarkar, Profulla C. 1982. "Customs and Beliefs Associated with Sexual Behavior and Human Fertility in Rural Bangladesh." *Eastern Anthropologist* 35: 135–42.

Schacht, Joseph. 1964. *An Introduction to Islamic Law.* Oxford: Oxford University Press.

Schieffelin, Olivia, ed. 1972. *Muslim Attitudes Toward Family Planning.* New York: Population Council.

Siddiqui, M. K. A. 1968. "Family Planning: The Islamic Point of View." *Family Planning News* (July): 2–4.

Sodhy, L. S., Gale A. Metcalf, and Joel S. Wallach. 1980. *Islam and Family Planning: Indonesia's Mohammadiyah.* Publication of the Pathfinder Fund, no. 6, edited by Ronald S. Waife. Chestnut Hill, Mass.: Pathfinder Fund.

Tashakkori, Abbas, Vaida D. Thompson, and Amir H. Mehryar. 1987. "Iranian Adolescents' Intended Age of Marriage and Desired Family Size." *Journal of Marriage and the Family* 49: 917–27.

Uche, U. U., ed. 1976. *Law and Population Change in Africa.* Nairobi, Kenya: East African Literature Bureau.

Waldman, Marilyn Robinson. 1985. Review of *Sex and Society in Islam: Birth Control before the Nineteenth Century,* by Basim F. Musallam. *Journal of Interdisciplinary History* 16(1): 173–5.

Warwick, Donald P. 1982. *Bitter Pills: Population Policies and Their Implementation in Eight Developing Countries.* New York: Cambridge University Press.

Winters, Clyde Ahmad. 1985. "Islam and Birth Control in Muslim Minority Areas of China." *Asian Thought and Society* 10(30): 179–85.

World Bank. 1990. *World Development Report 1990.* New York: Oxford University Press.

Youssef, Nadia. 1973. "Cultural Ideals, Feminine Behavior, and Family Control." *Comparative Studies in Society and History* 15(3): 326–47.

4

Islamic Law and Zakat: Waqf Resources in Pakistan[1]

Gail Richardson

Zakat is the obligatory transfer of a prescribed proportion of property by a Muslim who owns more wealth than the limit dictated under Islamic Law (*shari'a*). It is a pillar of faith and an act of worship that involves monetary and fiscal action. Literally, zakat is a 2.5 percent tax levied on certain assets, including savings accounts, gold, and silver. The funds collected are used for charitable activities to improve the living standards of poor Muslims, including the provision of health care and education.

Zakat is not considered charity. It is instead a clearly defined right of the poor members of the Muslim community to share in the wealth of those with more financial resources. The well-to-do (*sahib-e-nisab*) are obliged by their faith to give to the needy (*mustaheqeen*), and the Islamic state must ensure that this obligation is discharged. Islamic society views poverty and destitution as social conditions that should be actively addressed, and priority is given to ensuring a just and dignified life for every member of society. This unparalleled solution for eliminating poverty establishes the principle that national wealth is a "trust" (*amanat*) from Allah and has to be acquired and disbursed in accordance with the moral and social values of Islam. By spending his or her wealth according to Allah's will, a person receives Allah's promise of bounteous rewards for these noble acts.

Since the advent of Islam in 622 C.E., zakat has been practiced in Islamic countries. Since then, the payment of zakat continues, especially where there are governments that follow Islamic principles, although the arrangements for collection and distribution may differ. Saudi Arabia, the seat of Islam since the beginning, follows zakat to the letter. Other countries (e.g., Bangladesh, Kuwait, Malaysia, and Sudan) collect zakat on a voluntary basis. In Pakistan, zakat was voluntary from August 1947 until 1980, when zakat became law, conferring its benefits to over 13.52 million people from 1980 to 1990. The Constitution of Pakistan, a state established in the name of Islam, includes provisions for the proper organization of zakat.

Zakat Resources in Pakistan

SOURCES OF INCOME

Assets that are subject to zakat are divided into two broad categories: those subject to compulsory levy and those subject to self-assessment. Assets subject to compulsory levy through deduction-at-source for deposit into the Central Zakat Fund are savings bank accounts and similar accounts; notice deposit and similar accounts and receipts; fixed deposit and similar accounts and receipts on which the return is receivable by the holder periodically or is received earlier than maturity or withdrawal; savings deposit and similar certificates, accounts, and receipts on which return is receivable and is received by the holder only on maturity or when redeemed; National Investment Trust Units; Investment Corporation of Pakistan mutual fund certificates; government securities on which the return is receivable by the holder periodically; securities including shares and debentures of companies and statutory corporations on which return is paid; annuities; life insurance policies; and Provident Fund credit balances.

Zakat is collected from every sahib-e-nisab on a compulsory basis[2] each year starting on the first day of Ramadan, at the rates and in the manner specified on the valuation date (i.e., first of Ramadan for the whole of the preceding zakat year) at the rates and in the manner specified by the Central Zakat Council.

Assets subject to self-assessment are items that are not subject to compulsory levy of zakat but on which zakat is payable by every sahib-e-nisab. This payment can be made either to a zakat fund or to any individual or institution eligible under shari'a to receive zakat. The items subject to self-assessment include gold, silver, and derivatives thereof; cash; prize bonds; current accounts; loans receivable; securities, including shares and debentures not liable to compulsory levy; stock-in-trade of commercial undertakings, industrial undertakings, precious metals, stones, and derivatives thereof, and fish and other catch/produce of the sea; agricultural produce not liable to compulsory *ushr* levy; animals fed free in pasture (goats, sheep, cows, buffalos, camels); and other items not specified in the two schedules but liable to zakat under shari'a.

USES OF FUNDS

Zakat money may be used for the following purposes: First, funds may be used to provide assistance to the needy, the indigent and the poor (particularly orphans and widows), the handicapped and the disabled, and those eligible to receive zakat under shari'a for subsistence or rehabilitation, either directly or indirectly through madrassas, vocational educational institutions, public hospitals, clinics, dispensaries, or health laboratories. Second, zakat can be used for administrative expenses on an extremely selective basis; as a rule, these expenditure are financed by the government or agencies concerned. Third, funds may be allocated for any other purpose permitted by shari'a.

The level of zakat funds collected on a compulsory basis showed an annual growth of over 11 percent from 1980–1990.[3] Out of the total Rs 9625.33 million distributed from FY81 to FY90 (1400–1410 A.H.) to the provinces of Punjab, Sindh, NWFP (North West Frontier Province), Balochistan, and Islamabad

Capital Territory, and through them to the district and local zakat committees (LZCs), Rs 7895.62 million was disbursed. Over 13.5 million needy people benefited through support provided for subsistence, religious schools (*madrassas*), other educational institutions, and social welfare and health institutions. The Central Zakat Council is also financing the construction of two houses per LZC for the needy. Under this program about seventy-five thousand houses will be financed by the Zakat Fund at a cost of Rs 814.35 million. In addition, Rs 70.33 million has been allocated to national health institutions. Finally, Rs 165.49 million has been given as grants for emergencies.

Health and Education Sectors. In FY90, Rs 64.19 million (U.S. $2.97 million) was allocated to the health sector through the zakat program, which amounts to 4 percent of the FY90 federal government's budget for the health sector (Rs 1458.6 million). Of the total provincial zakat funds' budget, the proportion allocated for medical care increased from 6 percent in FY81 to 8 percent in FY90. In addition, the Central Zakat administration proposed an increase in the allocation of funds to the provincial funds from Rs 150 to Rs 200 per indigent. This revised allocation should increase the proportion of funds designated for health care from the current 8 percent to 20 percent of the provincial zakat funds' budget (of the Rs 640 million [U.S. $25.64 million] to be made available to the provinces in FY92, Rs 128 million (U.S. $5.13 million) is to be allocated for health care).

The Central Zakat Council's guidelines specify that 40 percent of the funds retained by the provincial councils are to be used for stipends and scholarships for formal education. Of the programs supported by provincial funds, the budget for scholarships was less than 1 percent of the total provincial budget in FY81 and 20 percent in FY90. The provincial zakat councils' allocation for postprimary scholarships and stipends increased from Rs 44,000 in FY81 (U.S. $4,467), or Rs 746 per beneficiary, to Rs 58.53

million in FY90 (U.S. $2.71 million), or Rs 2,081 per beneficiary. With the increase in funds from the Central Zakat Council, the proportion of funds designated for formal education should increase from the current 20 percent to 40 percent of the provincial zakat councils' budget.

Management of Funds. The 1980 Zakat and Ushr Ordinance provided for a five-tiered organizational structure to manage zakat funds: the Central Zakat Council at the central level; provincial zakat councils in the four provinces; a zakat committee in each district; *tehsil/taluka* akat ushr committee in each subdivision of Lahore district and Karachi division; and a local zakat committee for each block of three thousand to five thousand persons in urban areas and in each village (*deh*) in rural areas.

The Central Zakat Council provides policy guidelines for supervising all matters relating to zakat. The chair of the Central Zakat Council is a judge of the Supreme Court of Pakistan. Other members of the council include three religious leaders (*'ulama*) belonging to different schools of Islamic law (*fiqh*) and five public persons, at least one from each province. In addition, the federal secretaries of the Finance and Religious Affairs Division, the administrator-general, zakat, and the four provincial chief administrators, zakat, are ex-officio members.

A provincial zakat council has been constituted in each province with a sitting or retired judge of the High Court as chairman. The remaining nine members of the council include five public persons of whom three are religious leaders. Provincial cecretaries of Finance, Local Government, and Social Welfare Departments and the provincial chief administrators, zakat, are ex-officio members.

The chairman of the district zakat committee is a nonofficial person from the district nominated by the provincial council. Five other nonofficial members are nominated by the provincial council in consultation with the nominated chairman. The deputy commissioner of the district and a member nominated by the district council are the other two members. A tehsil/taluka zakat committee consists of six members elected from among the chairmen of the local zakat committees of the tehsil/taluka, a member nominated by the tehsil council and the assistant commissioner (*tehsildar/mukhtiarkar*). Chairmen and members of the district, tehsil, and local zakat committees, numbering over 292,000 people, work on a voluntary basis.

Zakat funds have been established at three levels: the Central Zakat Fund at the central level; a provincial zakat fund in each of the four provinces; and local zakat funds at the local level (one in each of the 38,800 localities). The major source of income into the Central Zakat Fund is the zakat deducted at source.[4] The funds transferred from the Central Zakat Fund are he major source of income for the provincial zakat funds. Most of the resources of the Local Zakat Funds are provided by the Provincial Zakat Fund; these funds, as a rule, stay in the locality where they are collected.

The custody of the Central Zakat Fund and of the four provincial zakat funds is with the central bank (the State Bank of Pakistan); that of the local zakat funds with the branches of the five nationalized banks (Habib Bank Limited, United Bank Limited, National Bank of Pakistan, Muslim Commercial Bank, and the Allied Bank of Pakistan Limited).[5]

An elaborate system of accounting for zakat funds at all three levels has been devised and is, by and large, being observed throughout the country. Qualified persons audit the Central Zakat Fund and the Provincial Zakat Funds. In addition, the Auditor-General of Pakistan audits the funds.[6]

COLLECTING ZAKAT

Banks, post offices, savings centers, and other banking and financial institutions in the country, with over fifteen thousand branches, serve as zakat collection agencies and offices without charging for their work. Moreover, the administrative expenses of the zakat organization, though chargeable to zakat funds according to the shari'a, are not charged to the Central Zakat Fund or provincial funds but are paid by the respective governments. This allows maximum use of zakat moneys for the needy.

Disbursing Zakat Funds. The Central Zakat Council has set the following guidelines for disbursing zakat: The provincial zakat councils retain 40 percent of the amount received from the Central Zakat Fund; the remaining 60 percent is transferred to the local zakat committees in the province. The provincial zakat councils can use their funds for stipends and scholarships through educational institutions (50 percent); stipends through madrassas (20 percent); medical aid through hospital and dispensaries (10 percent); assistance through social welfare institutions (10 percent); and other purposes (10 percent). Local zakat committees may use yearly zakat funds for rehabilitation (at least 45 percent); subsistence (not more than 45 percent); and administrative expenses (not more than 10 percent). The provincial zakat councils and local zakat committees adhere to these averages to the extent possible.

Zakat for subsistence and direct rehabilitation of individuals (by way of small business, etc.) is provided by the local zakat committees. The local zakat committee identifies and verifies the needs of the poor and decides when assistance should end. Priority is given to orphans, widows, the handicapped, the disabled, and students of religious schools. Needy students pursuing higher studies in medicine, engineering, accounting, commerce, and other disciplines are also eligible for zakat aid. Rehabilitation of the needy by the provincial zakat council is primarily through institutions.

FUTURE PLANS

The Central Zakat Council met in September 1991 to make decisions for the release of the twenty-fourth six-month installment of the Zakat Fund. The council's decisions included the following: (1) The current biannual installment of Rs 800 million to the provincial zakat funds was increased to Rs 960 million to cover the increased subsistence allowance per needy person from Rs 150 to Rs 200 per month.(2) Lists of needy persons will be prepared after verification of the financial status of the applicants. Priority is to be given to the indigent, widows, orphans, and handicapped to ensure that zakat money is spent on the needy. (3) Zakat committees will be reconstituted to enable the induction of two women in each local zakat committee to provide adequate representation to women in about 38,800 local zakat committees all over the country. (4) Funds will be provided for needy patients undergoing treatment in the National Institute of Heart Diseases and the Fauji Foundation. (The Fauji Foundation has provided artificial limbs to more than two thousand needy people from zakat funds). (5) The jurisdiction of the 1980 Zakat and Ushr Ordinance will be extended to the underdeveloped Northern Areas to benefit a large section of the population by providing subsistence and rehabilitation through education and training. The council has allocated Rs 25 million to the Northern Areas Zakat Council for financial assistance to the needy.

REFORMS IN THE ZAKAT SYSTEM

The prime minister of Pakistan recognized the need to improve the zakat system and a committee was appointed in September 1991 to review issues and provide recommendations. The general public and the officers and staff of the zakat administration were asked to suggest ways to streamline the zakat system in accordance with the Qur'an.

National Zakat Foundation

Islamic law states that zakat resources are for use by the poor directly; therefore, zakat funds cannot finance capital expenditures incurred by an institution serving the poor. To supplement the funding program specified under shari'a, the government of Pakistan established the National Zakat Foundation (NZF) in 1982. The foundation works toward the rehabilitation of the indigent by aiding relevant existing institutions and by establishing and managing new institutions. The foundation supports projects all over Pakistan, with at least one project in each district.

SOURCES OF INCOME

Using non-zakat funds, the government allocated Rs 100 million (U.S. $8.48 million) as an endowment to the foundation, and since 1982 the government has provided an additional Rs 75 million (U.S. $3.13 million). The foundation has provided project specific grants-in-aid totaling Rs 126 million (U.S. $5.25 million), and Rs 55 million remains in the budget for future allocation.

USES OF FUNDS

NZF provides grants-in-aid for construction of buildings, purchase of equipment and furniture, and purchase of vehicles by voluntary social-welfare institutions that fulfill certain conditions. Since 1986, over 60 percent of the funds allocated by the NZF have been for the health sector. General hospitals, specialized hospitals, and dispensaries are the primary institutions receiving funds. The remaining 40 percent is allocated to training institutions, including special education programs for the disabled. Training programs are solely for the development of a marketable skill (i.e., sewing, candle making, carpentry, etc.) and do not include formal or religious education. This budget breakdown represents a shift from 1982 through 1986, when 64 percent was allocated for training programs and 26 percent went to medical facilities (the remaining 10 percent was put in a "multipurpose" category). This shift is attributed to the completion of a large training program in Balochistan in 1986.

NZF does not give grants-in-aid for projects that do not have a charitable purpose (e.g., grants are given for support to the poor, education, medical treatment, and similar types of support but not religious teaching or worship) or for recurring expenses of the project (e.g., salaries, building maintenance, and cost of utilities). Out of 218 projects authorized during 1982–1991, the medical sector claimed 60, skills training 110, and special education and multipurpose 48. The share of the financing allocated to the health sector was 55 percent of total funds, followed by special education and multipurpose at 30 percent, and skills training (with the highest number of projects) claimed only 15 percent.

The foundation provides partial funding, and the project sponsors, who also administer the completed projects, provide additional funding; zakat funds, individual donations, and other sources of revenue are also used. Some of the allocations were canceled because beneficiaries could not fulfill their commitments to the NZF.

MANAGEMENT OF FUNDS

The NZF is an autonomous organization and statutory body of the ministry of finance. The Committee of Administration, headed by the minister of finance, formulates policy. The committee is bound by government directives on operations and the expenditure of funds, except for money received from the Zakat Fund, in which case the committee follows the Central Zakat Council. The Committee of Administration is empowered to purchase, sell, or otherwise deal in any sort of securities; raise loans for its undertakings and, for this purpose, to pledge, mortgage, or otherwise use the assets of the foundation; enter into contracts or arrangements and execute necessary documents; open bank accounts of any sort as necessary and pay into and withdraw from those accounts; and use checks, orders, promissory notes, and other sorts of negotiable instruments.

The Executive Committee, below the Committee of Administration, is headed by the secretary of finance and oversees the implementation of policy. In each of the four provinces, provincial subcommittees assist in the selection of projects for approval.

The federal government appoints a managing director of the foundation on such terms and conditions and for such periods as it may deem fit. The managing director works under the supervision, control, and guidance of the committee. As secretary and chief executive, the managing director is responsible for day-to-day administration and management.

The foundation may receive from the government or other bodies or persons grants, loans, donations, or contributions; receive, use, and disburse money from a zakat fund in accordance with the 1980 Zakat and Ushr Ordinance and shari'a; use the assets and the income of the foundation for NZF purposes; defray administrative costs, charges, and expenses; and take other necessary steps to attain NZF objectives.

THE NZF'S RELATIONSHIP WITH NONGOVERNMENTAL ORGANIZATIONS (NGOs)

The NZF provides grants primarily to NGOs since NGOs are in a better position than a government agency to respond to the needs of the community. The foundation's policy is to fund projects on a fifty-fifty cost-sharing basis with NGOs in urban areas. In rural areas, the NGO is responsible for 25 percent of the funds. In some cases an NGO will receive a grant and be asked to repay the funds in kind, that is, by providing services to the poor. To receive funds, the NGO must be a charitable institution aimed at the rehabilitation of the poor, be in operation and registered under the Voluntary Social Welfare Agencies Ordinance of 1961, demonstrate the financial means to support recurrent expenditures, and be able to support the cost-sharing component of the project.

The NGO is responsible for submitting periodic reports on the use of grant funds, progress reports on the authorized project, and reports on expenditures and receipts. Funds provided by the NZF must be kept in a separate account. The officers of the NZF and the provincial social welfare departments periodically inspect NZF-assisted projects to ensure proper use of the grant-in-aid and services. The completed projects are evaluated to assess whether the results were commensurate with expectations.

NZF GRANT-IN-AID APPLICATIONS

The NZF reviews projects for which grant-in-aid is requested to judge eligibility, whether the financial and managerial resources of the organization proposed to run the proposed project are adequate, and the need of the locality for the services proposed. Projects fulfilling the prescribed conditions and requiring grant-in-aid up to Rs 2 million are approved by the provincial subcommittee of the province in which the project is located. Projects requiring grant-in-aid of Rs 2 million up to Rs 5 million are approved by the Executive Committee. Projects requiring grant-in-aid of more than Rs 5 million are approved by the Committee of Administration.

DISBURSING GRANT-IN-AID

Grant-in-aid is disbursed to the applicant organization in installments that suit the projects. Grant-in-aid required for construction is released in installments to fit the time schedule and progress of construction; grant-in-aid for purchase of equipment can be made in a lump sum after acceptance of the lowest bid by the managing community.

The government of Pakistan has allocated a total budgetary grant of Rs 174.50 million (nonlapsable) from FY83–92. The number and size of the projects authorized depend on the respective shares of the provinces and the Islamabad Capital Territory. Priority is given to viable and eligible larger-scale projects.

FUTURE PLANS

Since many of the targeted NGOs are in remote areas, the foundation announces the availability of funds through periodic releases and limited advertising in various newspapers and journals. Word-of-mouth also plays an important role. In the subdistricts, the social welfare departments distribute application materials. The foundation is currently planning "Phase 2," which focuses on more effectively marketing the availability of funds.

Waqf Resources in Pakistan

The institution of *waqf* stems from the Islamic concept that money should be spent on establishing a social system that ensures the enduring welfare of the people. The best and most enduring form of spending money in the way of Allah, according to Islamic tradition and teachings, is waqf.

According to the Punjab Waqf Properties Ordinance IV of 1979, waqf is the permanent dedication, by a person professing Islam, of property of any kind for any purpose recognized as religious, pious, or charitable. The property, in effect, then belongs to Allah. The reward for an individual's kindness and generosity is Allah's favor in this world and in the hereafter. The consciousness in the Islamic world about accountability before Allah and about the responsibility to look after the needs of fellow human beings enabled the Muslim society to give the concept of public welfare a concrete shape through *awqaf* (sometimes *auwaf*; plural of waqf).

The first waqf was established in Madina when Hazrat Talha donated one of his gardens with a well as a trust. This concern for the common good set in motion a universal movement for establishment of awqaf. This practice provided a strong and stable basis for works of public welfare. In a short time, there was a proliferation of mosques, religious institutions, hospitals and houses for the poor, food for the unemployed, drinking water for travelers, and wells for irrigating farm lands. Institutions for the care of the handicapped and destitute children were formed, in addition to educational institutions, orphanages, houses for widows, veterinary hospitals, and organizations for the construction and upkeep of roads and bridges.

There are three types of awqaf recognized by law: the public waqf, for example, mosque, bridge, public road, and so forth; the semipublic waqf, for instance, a hospital for handicapped people, a school for non-Muslims, and so on; and the private waqf, which serves the interest of the descendants of an individual. Once a property is made into a waqf it remains a waqf for perpetuity. The property cannot be given, sold, or inherited. Anything that can be owned may be subject to waqf: land, books, shops, money, animals, trees, and more. For a waqf to be valid, the subject matter must be the full property of the donor and the beneficiaries must be described fully.

Waqf property includes property used for any purpose recognized by Islam as religious, pious, or charitable. Waqf property also includes boxes placed at a shrine and offerings presented to a shrine or to any person on the premises of a shrine; property permanently dedicated for the purposes of a mosque, *takia*, *khankah*, *dargah*, or other shrine; and relief for the poor and orphans, education, workshop, medical relief, maintenance of shrines, or any other charitable, religious, or pious purposes.

The waqf system has furthered economic, social, and cultural development in Muslim societies. Built on a religious foundation to provide for the needy and to contribute to public welfare, waqf is designed to work in and for the community without any interference from the state (the judicial system that administers it is independent from the state), which conforms with the decentralized nature of Islamic law.

The institution of waqf could be and was at times abused at the hands of the state and unscrupulous administrators or judges who did not follow the letter of the law. After the colonial mandates eliminated the institution of waqf, the postmandate states retained the colonial policies of eliminating the communal and private awqaf in many fields and establishing state (rather than community) control over the institutions involved, which was precisely what Islamic law sought to avoid. In most of the Arab near East, only a few types of awqaf survive, although the pressure of the electorate has resulted in restoration of the institution in many countries in recent years.

SOURCES OF INCOME

Individuals who have founded awqaf include kings, scholars, physicians, leaders, soldiers, government officials, peasants, industrialists, traders, and all people of wealth. Income accrues from waqf properties in the form of donations by the general public, lease money of lands or plots, rent of houses, shops, and so forth. Revenues for FY91 were Rs 86.07 million (U.S. $3.63 million), 57 percent of which came from cash donations at shrines, 12 percent from leases on agricultural lands, 16 percent from rental property, and 14 percent from miscellaneous sources. The entire income is credited to the Central Auqaf Fund, which is maintained by the National Bank of Pakistan, Al-Shajjar Branch, Nila Gumbad, Lahore. The Bank consolidates the income through its branches in the province. A chief administrator manages the Central Auqaf Fund in accordance with the Punjab Waqf Properties Ordinance of 1979.

USES OF FUNDS

Schools and colleges; institutions of education, science, and research; libraries; hospitals; medical schools; study circles; and seminaries have been created in large numbers in many parts of the Islamic world, including Egypt, Iran, Iraq, Morocco, Pakistan, Syria, and Turkey. Most of these institutions owe their existence to individual awqaf. The biggest university in Damascus, Syria, was established as a waqf, and many hospitals and medicals schools were set up by kings and court officials as individual awqaf. Unlike similar trusts in other nations, the Islamic waqf seeks much wider goals. Waqf resources are not confined to the building of places of worship, educational institutions, or the support of the poor; funds also support the health sector. The use of waqf funds is also not confined to a particular race or religion and includes mental as well as physical welfare.

HEALTH AND EDUCATION SECTORS

The Auqaf Department has been increasing annual contributions to the health and education sectors. The investment in the health sector has increased nominally from Rs 7.66 million in FY86 (U.S. $0.46 million) to Rs 12.23 million (U.S. $0.49 million) in FY92 (budget). In FY91, Rs 10.19 million (U.S. $0.43 million), 11 percent of the total provincial budget, was allocated to the health sector. Data Darbar Hospital Complex, Lahore, which provides free medical care and numerous dispensaries, is the main achievement of the Auqaf Department in the health sector. Waqf funds also support eighteen religious education schools in Punjab, attended by five thousand students.

MANAGEMENT OF FUNDS

The ministry of religious affairs manages the waqf funding program at the national level. At the provincial level, the Auqaf Department manages and develops waqf properties. In the province of Punjab, the work involves: legislation, organizational setup, rules about the provision of services, and managing income from and expenditure on waqf properties and development projects. There had not been legislation at the state level empowering the government to administrate, manage, or control waqf properties. However, in 1977, to correct mismanagement of funds, the government of Pakistan federalized the provincial auqaf departments. Then, in 1979, the government defederalized the management and administration of waqf properties. The Punjab Waqf Properties Ordinance was promulgated in 1979, making the Auqaf Department autonomous. The objectives of the Auqaf Department are to administer, manage, and control waqf properties to ensure better management of income-yielding properties attached to shrines and mosques or otherwise dedicated to religious or charitable purposes; improve the standards of religious services and rights and the maintenance of the mosques and shrines; make the holy places centers of cultural and spiritual regeneration for Muslims in accordance with the dictates of Islam; eradicate antisocial, immoral, and irreligious practices at holy places; and ensure that the income from waqf properties is used for purposes recognized by Islam as religious, pious, or charitable. Other objectives are to ensure proper administration, control, management, and maintenance of properties taken over by the awqaf organization through mandatory instructions of a government-appointed officer to persons in charge of properties under the control of the awqaf; to improve religious education from elementary school to the university; to encourage teaching of the Qur'an and provide training to persons in charge of waqf facilities.

The Auqaf Department is headed by a secretary who is also chief administrator. The chief administrator is in charge of administration and management of all waqf properties in the province. The Auqaf Department has zonal offices in the divisional headquarters and a properties section at the head office. On the government side, the secretary of the Auqaf Department is assisted by an officer on special duty and other subordinate staff who conduct government business relating to awqaf and the communities. The zonal administrators do surveys of the waqf properties in their zones, which they send to the property section of the head office. The surveys are examined and the chief administrator assumes responsibility for income-yielding waqf properties.

Traditionally, the waqf properties comprise shrines, mosques, shops, and agricultural lands. The officials in charge of the management of shrines and the administration of mosques are accountable to the respective district managers of awqaf. The district manager is also responsible for auctioning the leases of lands and renting out the shops and houses. The district managers are accountable to zonal administrators. Administrators, in turn, are accountable to the administrator of awqaf at headquarters.

The Auqaf Department has a project directorate that deals with the planning, designing, and execution of works. The directorate has two wings. One, headed by director, projects (conservation), deals with the conservation of historic monuments. Three subdivisional officers and allied engineering staff assist the director. Conservation work is executed by department engineers. The other wing of the directorate is headed by the director, projects auqaf, who supervises new projects and the maintenance of mosques, shrines, and buildings.

Accountability. The budget, audit, and accounts of the Auqaf Department are governed by Waqf Properties (Accounts) Rules, 1960. The budget estimates for the ensuing year are prepared by the assistant managers of the Auqaf Department who submit these estimates to the respective zonal administrators. The zonal administrators review and consolidate the budgets for the chief administrator. The budgets of all zones/offices are reviewed by the chief administrator and are sent to the financial advisor of awqaf, who is also the additional secretary (budget) for the Finance Department of the government of Punjab. After the financial advisor reviews the budget, the chief administrator convenes an administrator's conference at headquarters for a comparative study of various zonal budgets. This meeting is attended by all the zonal administrators of awqaf, the financial advisor, the administrator of awqaf, Punjab, and all the section officers. The budget is recast in the light of decisions made at the conference. The budget is then submitted for approval to the Subject Committee for Awqaf of the province.

Future Plans. In September 1991, the Secretary and chief administrator recommended increasing support for health services as resources become available.

National Evacuee Trust Property Board

Unlike zakat and waqf, which are Islamic concepts, the National Evacuee Trust Property Board (NETPB) is a separate institutional setup. The NETPB was established to take over the administration of trusts previously established by the Hindus and Sikhs who left Pakistan in 1947. While the board's primary responsibility is to maintain the religious shrines of the Sikhs and Hindus, the NETPB also provides social services to the community, with a focus on the health and education sectors. The board finances six dispensaries, a school, and several research facilities. Projects in the planning stages include a 150-bed maternal and pediatric hospital and a Rs 50 million (U.S. $2.0 million) endowment and land for the Pakistan Model Education Institutions Foundation, a project to set up model schools in several cities.

In FY91, the NETPB's expenditure on health services was Rs 3.73 million (U.S. $0.16 million), which amounts to less than 1 percent of the federal government's budget for the health sector in FY91 (Rs 2410.5 million). However, for FY92 a substantial increase in funding is planned. Rs 4.30 million will be allocated for continued financing of health projects (e.g., six dispensaries), and approximately Rs 10.4 million will be allocated for grants-in-aid to various health institutions, bringing the total FY92 health sector budget to Rs 14.7 million (U.S. $0.59 million).

SOURCES OF INCOME

The NETPB generates incomes from the sale and leasing of property and from investments in securities.

USES OF FUNDS

The main objective of the board is maintenance of religious shrines and provision of facilities for pilgrims. For this purpose, the budget provides funds under the heading "Repair to Shrines and Festivals." In the 1990–1991 budget, Rs 1.4 million was provided for repairs to shrines and Rs 3.3 million for festivals, including facilities for pilgrims.

The second most important objective of the board is grants-in-aid for social welfare, education, health institutions, and hospitals. Prior to 1988–1989, Rs 4.5 million was provided in the budget for extending grant-in-aid to these fields. Since 1988, Rs 6.5 million has been provided. In 1991, a recurring annual grant of Rs 2.5 million was allocated to the following institutions in the Punjab, NWFP, and Balochistan: Gulab Devi Hospital, Ganga Ram Hospital, Janki Devi Hospital, Tibbia College, Research Society of Pakistan at Lahore, University of Peshawar (for research), and Lady Dufferin Hospital at Quetta. The remaining Rs 4.0 million was allocated for nonrecurring grants. In the budget for 1991, the federal government increased grant-in-aid from Rs 6.5 million to Rs 13.0 million.

An analysis of the NETPB grants-in-aid from 1977–1978 to 1989–1990 shows:

a. The province share is highest for Punjab (82 percent). Prepartition trust institutions in Lahore, particularly in the health sector, such as Ghulab Devi Hospital, Ganga Ram Hospital, and Janki Devi Hospital, but also in other sectors, such as the Dyal Singh Trust Library, receive grants-in-aid regularly for renovation and expansion to cater to the growing needs of the population.

b. Looking at the breakdown of grants-in-aid by sector, a similar pattern has emerged in favor of the health sector (73.4 percent), followed by education (13.8 percent), social welfare (9.5 percent), and miscellaneous (3.3 percent). As noted above, the reason for the higher levels of grants for the health sector is due to the support provided to a number of hospitals that date from prepartition days.

Health and Education Sectors. The board maintains several health and education institutions. Six health centers have been set up under the auspices of the board—four at Lahore, one at Nankana

Sahib, and one at Hassanabdal. These centers offer medical services to the local populace and pilgrims. The annual expenditure is Rs 0.9 million. The board has also set aside a valuable piece of trust land, measuring about thirty *kanals* (approximately four acres), in the densely populated area of Misri Shah, Lahore, for construction of a hospital for the care of mothers and children. In the education sector, Dayal Singh Trust Library is a main library in Punjab, catering to general readers as well as research scholars. The annual expenditure for the library is Rs 2.34 million. Additionally, an education foundation has been set up in Lahore under orders of the prime minister. The foundation aims to set up model institutions in important cities of Pakistan. A grant of Rs 50 million, along with valuable property, has been given to the foundation.

MANAGEMENT OF FUNDS

Evacuee trust property was managed by the Custodian/Settlement Organization from 1947 to 1960. The federal government then constituted a board for the management and disposal of these properties under the Displaced Persons Act. In 1975, the Evacuee Trust Properties Act provided "for the management and disposal of evacuee properties attached to charitable, religious or educational trusts or institutions." The board is a corporate body with power to hold moveable and immovable property. It supervises and controls all evacuee trust property under the direction of the federal government. The chairman of the board decides whether the evacuee property is attached to a charitable, religious, or educational trust. Any person aggrieved can appeal to the chairman or to the government. The board consists of twenty-four members from all provinces. One member is from the Hindu community while four members represent the federal government: joint secretary, ministry of interior; joint secretary and financial advisor, ministry of religious affairs and minorities affairs; and joint secretary, ministry of health and special education. The board headquarters are in Lahore. For effective management of the properties, which are scattered throughout Pakistan, evacuee trust property offices have been set up at district and zone levels, with field offices in Karachi, Multan, Lahore, and Rawalpindi.

The NETPB has broad responsibilities. The board maintains complete records of properties; prepares a budget; buys property using surplus income and proceeds from disposal/sale and transfer of properties (with the approval of the federal government); leases property; assesses rent and lease money; repairs and maintains shrines of evacuees; provides grants-in-aid for social welfare, education, and health institutions; undertakes development programs; invests surplus funds in securities and institutions; and defends suits and proceedings in the courts of law.

The board manages two types of properties: agricultural land and urban property (houses, shops, and open sites). The lease of evacuee trust agricultural land is regulated by the Scheme for the Lease of Evacuee Trust Agricultural Land 1975, and the tenancy/lease of urban properties is regulated by the Scheme for the Management and Disposal of Urban Evacuee Trust Properties 1977.

FUTURE PLANS

NETPB plans to invest its significant resources (financial and property) to expand the country's health care, education, and social welfare network, including (*a*) a 150-bed Hospital at Lahore at an estimated cost of Rs 40 million; proposals for new dispensaries and health facilities in Karachi (one hospital), Sukhur and Hyderabad (one dispensary each), Quetta (two dispensaries), Rawalpindi (one hospital), Peshawar (one dispensary), and Khushab (one large dispensary) and for family planning clinics; (*b*) donation of a large piece of property to the Pakistan Model Education Institutions Foundation, Lahore, with a one-time cash grant of Rs 50 million; and (*c*) increased investment in health care and education in urban and rural areas. The NETPB has both land

and staff in rural areas of the country; the basis for an infrastructure in the remote areas already exists.

Overall Issues and Recommendations

The main issues that have arisen about the zakat funding program are (a) the lack of clarity with respect to the relations with other public institutions such as the health facilities financed by the ministry of public health; (b) few checks and balances in fund allocation to prevent misappropriation; (c) allocation based on the general population, rather than on the indigent population; (d) lack of follow-up on an individual's eligibility; and (e) limited follow-up on the proper use of funds earmarked for rehabilitation.

Recommendations for a more effective program include (a) ensuring coordination with services provided by other public and nongovernmental organizations; (b) improving management of funds; (c) implementing more extensive quality control; and (d) analyzing program effectiveness to ensure that funds are properly used to meet the needs of the poor.

Issues concerning the NZF include the following: (a) as with the use of zakat resources, the link between the institutions financed by the NZF and other publicly-financed institutions is not clear; (b) the effectiveness of marketing the availability of funds (as well as maintaining appropriate financial accounts) is questionable, particularly given the high illiteracy rates in Pakistan; (c) there is a lack of formal management and record keeping training for the NGOs; and (d) project effectiveness analysis is not sufficiently strong nor fully integrated into the operations of the NZF.

Recommendations for improving the effectiveness of the NZF include (a) enhancing the link with other public institutions; (b) improving the marketing strategies; (c) upgrading management skills and record keeping through training programs; and (d) analyzing project effectiveness to improve the management of funds.

The following issues have arisen from this preliminary study of awqaf in Pakistan: (a) there is limited analysis of program effectiveness, especially with regard to the management of resources and responsiveness to the needs of the poor; (b) there is a lack of formal management training; and (c) there is a possible need to change current management techniques and project implementation systems.

Recommendations to improve the waqf system include: (a) conducting an impact assessment to ascertain the effect of grant-in-aid on the health, education, and social welfare of the needy and to target new areas for improvement; (b) expanding the network of dispensaries, health centers, and hospitals to overcome inadequate health care services; (c) ensuring equity in the distribution of funds, particularly in rural areas; and (d) improving management training and project implementation systems.

The main recommendations that have arisen from this preliminary analysis are that coordination with other publicly financed services and institutions be ensured, the sustainability and quality of the programs supported through the grants-in aid be analyzed, and a longer term for the chairman of the NETPB (currently appointed for a three-year term) be considered as a way to facilitate greater continuity of program policies and procedures.

Conclusions

Although the expenditures on health are not large in relative terms (5 percent of all expenditures), it is expected that they have increased since the time that this study was completed. Health status in Pakistan remains poor along a number of key variables. It is therefore paramount that sectoral resources are spent cost effectively and are well targeted to ensure maximum impact. This underscores the importance of coordination and collaboration with the primary financiers and providers of health services, such as the ministry of health.

This study provides only a glimpse into the resources and

management of these Islamic institutions and the NETPB. It is neither current nor complete. However, it makes clear that partners working to strengthen the health sector in Pakistan would be wise to include these organizations in their analysis and programs. From a social, political, and economic perspective, these institutions warrant involvement. They provide and finance important social services in Pakistan, and their role is growing.

Notes

1. Data and information were gathered from public documents and other materials in 1991.
2. A number of registered companies do not pay zakat, and there is a trend that some bond and saving schemes are also exempted from zakat or zakat is made voluntary.
3. The amount collected during 140–11 A.H. (June 1990 to March 1991) was Rs 2705.53 million, an increase from previous years. This year was not included in this study because releases and disbursements down to the local zakat committee level were not available at the time the analysis was completed.
4. Zakat funds deducted "at source" are deposited into the Central Zakat Fund and are then distributed by the Central Zakat Council to several institutions operating on a national level (i.e., hospitals that serve a patient population greater than one province), and to the four provincial zakat councils, based on the population of the province.
5. Privatized in 1991.
6. Detailed statutory rules and procedures are explained in "The Zakat Manual," June 1982 (updated September 1989).

5

Islam and Health Policy: A Study of the Islamic Republic of Iran[1]

Carol Underwood

The Iranian revolution of 1979, inspired by Islamic precepts and presided over by Muslim religious figures, brought Islam to the forefront of social, political, and economic discussions. Subsequent events around the world, in which tragedies have far outweighed triumphs, have kept discussions and debate about Islam and development very much on the global agenda. Political pundits were forced to reformulate some of their conjectures about the Muslim world, while scholarly social critics were compelled to reassess their assumption that Islam as a sociopolitical force had outlived its potential. These events have also had practical consequences: Muslim leaders and development specialists began to reevaluate the influence—whether manifest or latent—of religious understandings, practices, and institutions on policy formation and implementation. While this reorientation has been far from complete, it provides a clear contrast to the middle decades of the twentieth century, when regimes throughout most of the Muslim world turned to nationalist or socialist rhetoric to garner (or maintain) legitimacy and sought to distance themselves from tradition and religion. The wide-ranging effect of this shift is too broad to explore in one study, but our understanding of how the explicit incorporation of religious principles has altered policy formation and implementation can be furthered through the analysis of postrevolutionary Iran.

The purpose of this chapter is to examine the impact of religious doctrine, as refracted through political discourse, on health policy in Iran. To provide a backdrop for this discussion, a brief profile of health policies prior to the revolution follows.

Prerevolutionary Health Policy

Social policy in developing nations is guided, though not necessarily determined, by the state's interpretation of the causes and prerequisites for development. Modernization theory was the dominant paradigm in development thought in the 1950s and 1960s. The central contention of modernization theory, which conceptualizes societies within a bipolar framework, is that development is a unidirectional evolutionary process as exemplified in the development of the modern West. Through the introduction of certain concepts and technological interventions, it was argued, development would take off—but this development should be controlled and incremental. This same approach was used in the fields of medicine and public health—health improvement was sought through technology and curative care rather than through broad changes in social and economic structures. The guiding principle was that traditional ways inhibited development: tradition was juxtaposed to "modernization." The Shah and his supporters were loyal proponents of the modernization perspective and often found themselves at odds with traditional leaders, including the Muslim 'ulama.

Cosmopolitan medicine was relatively well established among the urban elite by the 1960s. Medical schools had been established not only in Tehran, but also in many of the provincial capitals. As Iran became more thoroughly integrated into the world economy, foreign suppliers of medical technology, together with transnational pharmaceutical companies, increasingly influenced the practice of medicine in Iran. The inevitable struggle between public health specialists and private enterprise medicine saw the latter predominate, but the public health sector continued to act as a countervailing force.

Based upon lessons learned from China's experiences with primary health care (PHC), several pilot projects were undertaken in Iran in the 1970s. With the wholehearted support of Iran's major public health schools, health planners set out to test the capacity of rural health houses to provide basic preventive and curative care for the rural population. One major and very successful program was established in West Azerbaijan, where—significantly—there was no medical school to serve as the basis for opposition to the emphasis on primary care delivered by paraprofessionals.[2] Other effective projects were located in Shiraz, the provincial capital of Fars province, and among the Qashqa'i nomads. Rural health houses were linked to an urban hospital; there were no intermediary referral centers.

Despite these experiments with PHC, there was tenuous evidence, at best, that these services would be instituted nationwide (Andreano 1984). Indeed, the pilot projects faced stiff opposition from the medical establishment, including professors and deans of the leading medical schools, as well as from influential physicians, who argued that the "quality of care" would suffer. Geographically and temporally limited, the pilot projects had little effect on the population at large. As Andreano notes, "Provision of, and access to, health care in rural areas in 1978 was still where it was in 1973. One is left with the conclusion that the disparities that existed in social equity in 1978 were intensified and widened by national policy" (Andreano 1984, 5). For the rural population at large, modern medicine was typically introduced in the form of a mass campaign, with no permanent infrastructure to sustain health interventions (Assar and Jaksic 1975). Nevertheless, the experiments of the 1970s and the prototypes that had been developed earlier in China, among other places, provided experiences and guidelines that would prove vital to the implementation of a nationwide PHC network in the 1980s.

In the late 1970s, health care services in Iran were similar to those found in many technologically developing countries— highly sophisticated medical care for those in major metropolitan areas who could afford it concurrent with few services for the disadvantaged and rural populations. Health services were oriented toward curative care for the individual, with the hospital and technologically oriented medicine serving as the system's focal point. The majority of Iranians who lived in villages and who constituted approximately 50 percent of the total population lacked potable water supplies, basic sanitary services, immunization coverage, and any form of continuous primary care. The health system itself was less a "system" than a collection of over ninety agencies with fragmented and multiple delivery points whose services failed to reach the majority of the population (King 1983).

Medical education curricula, patterned after French, English, and, since World War II, American models, emphasized diseases prevalent in the West with little discussion of the health problems endemic in Iran. That the pattern of disease prevalence and incidence in Iran was significantly different from that seen in the industrialized world failed to influence the medical school curricula. Physician education was confined to the classroom and urban medical centers. There was little attempt to acquaint physician-trainees with the health problems of rural Iran. Indeed, even health bureaucrats avoided trips to rural areas. The explanation given by one such official was that "he knew what he was going to find, and therefore, there was no need to make the trip" (Ugalde 1978, 3). In an atmosphere dominated by urban concerns and curative care, prevention received little notice.

Without question, the West was upheld as the model to follow. A statement by the director of health planning of the Iranian ministry of health illustrates this in the field of medicine:

The best medical system in the world is the one of the United States. We are trying to do as there. In our country with a mixed economy the wealthy people will always be able to purchase better medical services than the poor [will]. We look at medical care as a privilege and not as a right. If we would look at health care as a right, then anybody could come and demand services, and we do not have resources in the government for that. (quoted in Ugalde 1978, 4; emphasis added)

Origins of Islamic Ideology

Before the mid-1970s, Islam seemed relatively quiescent outside the inner sanctum of the mosque, where adherence to Islamic rituals was the order of the day. Islam, it appeared, had been relegated to the private sphere, disinterested in public forums. While the students of Muslim countries knew of occasions in which the banner of Islam had been carried high to effect political ends, such as in the formation of the Muslim Brotherhood, the Iranian revolution made it dramatically clear that Islamic ideology or thought is today a vital social and political force. That revolution has come to symbolize, for believers and observers alike, the watershed event of the late twentieth century in the understanding and analysis of Islam.

The Iranian revolution is but the most striking manifestation of an ongoing transformative movement, the antecedents of which can be traced to nineteenth-century Muslim thinkers, that has redefined and reinvigorated Islam in recent decades. Quietistic tendencies that promised otherworldly salvation were gradually replaced with a worldview that promotes this-worldly activity to bring about a just society without relinquishing the promise of salvation. The interjection of a patently political and social lexicon into Islamic discourse reflected the growing tendency to view Islam as a total ideology that provides meaning and direction to all spheres of life. In other words, Islamic ideology encompasses an interpretive framework through which to view the world, together with guidelines to change social reality to conform to an ideal vision—an Islamic utopia.

It is more accurate to speak of Islamic ideologies, for just as there is not one monolithic understanding of Islam, there is more than one ideology espoused within the Muslim world. Moreover, ideological content and expression change over time and so are most productively viewed within a given historical period. In this paper, ideology will be used in the Mannheimian sense of "total conceptions of ideology," which he defines as "the ideology of an age or of a concrete historico-social group (e.g., of a class), when we are concerned with the characteristics and composition of the total structure of the mind of this epoch or of this group" (Mannheim 1936, 56). Ideology is understood to be socially and historically determined. It is important to note that this conceptualization of ideology does not equate ideology with false consciousness, as it has no denunciatory intent.

The definitive sources of Islamic doctrine are two: the Qur'an and the *Sunna*. The Qur'an comprises 114 suras, or chapters, revealed to the Prophet Muhammad from 610, the year of his call, until he died in 632. The Qur'an has been the source from which Muslims have derived not only their law and theology, but also principles and institutions of their public life. The term "Sunna" means the example or model for others to follow. The Sunna, therefore, purportedly gives us the precepts and actions of the Prophet Muhammad outside the Qur'an. These precepts and deeds are conveyed through the traditions (*hadith*).[3] Despite some strikingly disparate interpretations of Islam, the writings and lectures of every important twentieth-century Muslim visionary can be traced back to these sources.

Fazlur Rahman argues that the "extraordinary Qur'anic emphases on monotheism on the one hand and socioeconomic justice and egalitarianism on the other are organically linked—the Qur'an seems to proclaim one God, one humanity" (1987, 13).

The Qur'an enjoins believers to provide for the needs of the community: "Did you see the one who gives the lie to the faith? It is he who maltreats orphans and works little for the feeding of the poor. Woe betide, then, those who pray, yet are neglectful of their prayers" (107:1–7). And, "O You who believe! spend [for the poor] from the choicest part of your wealth" (3:92). This sense of the community and of a social ethic directly inspired the undertaking of works of social welfare, including health services.

Islamic Ideology in Contemporary Iran

The resonance of the signs and symbols embodied in Islamic discourse can be most fruitfully understood from the perspective of the participants themselves. Social and historical events of the late twentieth century created a situation in which contemporary movements in the Muslim world gained their sustenance from an idiom predominantly Islamic in tenor, rather than socialist or nationalist as had been the case earlier in the century. Muslims (re)turned to Islam, which they perceived as an authentic ideology that could liberate believers from foreign domination, whether in the economic or the cultural spheres.

Among the clergy, who in the 1960s saw the need to establish links between the Shi'ite center of learning in Qum and the secular universities, were Sayyid Mahmud Taliqani, Morteza Mutahhari, and Sayyid Muhammad Beheshti. These religious figures had an important influence on the evolution and dissemination of Islamic ideology in Iran. But it was the critical stance of Al-e Ahmad, an author and essayist, together with the views promulgated by Ali Shariati, a French-educated sociologist, that by the early 1970s inspired intellectuals to criticize the Shah's regime and its insistence that Iranians become socially and culturally westernized. While economic independence and political freedom constituted important aspects of their proposals, it was their call for a "return to the self" that struck a responsive chord in the Iranian psyche.

Shariati portrayed Shi'ism as a progressive, indigenous force that could embrace modernity—especially the scientific and technological advances—without relinquishing the spiritual, social, and moral principles of Islam. Economic development, he contended, could occur without tearing the social fabric.

The Qur'an and the traditions (hadith), it was argued, provided guidelines for every sphere of life, from the economic to the spiritual, from the political to the social. Shariati was able to reconstruct Shi'ite ideology as a revolutionary doctrine and use the mosque network in tandem with university forums to disseminate his central ideas. His message appealed to a significant sector of the nontraditional middle class, such as engineers, doctors, and white-collar employees. Much facilitated by Shariati's somewhat unique interpretations, the oppositional teachings of the 'ulama had gained salience among secular and religious intellectuals by the mid-1970s. Within a few years, the Shah's regime would lose its already tenuous legitimacy.

In postrevolutionary Iran, the previously oppositional discourse that informed the struggle against the old regime quickly became the dominant discourse and was used by the ruling elite to legitimate legislation as well as to enforce traditional mores. To understand how abstract principles can affect everyday life, this paper explores the role of Islamic thought in an applied field—namely, public health services, broadly defined.

Health Policy in the Islamic Republic of Iran

The Constitutional Law of the Islamic Republic of Iran calls for the "[a]doption of a sound, equitable economic policy according to the Islamic criteria with a view to ensuring public welfare, putting an end to destitution and indigence and deprivation as regards nourishment, housing, employment, health and insurance services" (Article 3). Moreover, it states that the "need for health and therapeutic services and medical care . . . shall be a right for all the people" (Article 29).

As part of the attempt to provide these services, the Iranian ministry of health began shortly after the revolution to reassess the needs of the population it served based on the tenets of Islam, as understood by the revolutionary government. It would be several years before health-policy changes were formally instituted, but early on the decision was made to increase health expenditures, particularly with respect to preventive and public health measures. Immunizations, potable water, and electricity for village inhabitants were given high priority. This reflects the regime's broad commitment to rural development and the improvement of the fortune of the peasantry (Arjomand 1988, 207). The efforts of the ministry of health were aided by other governmental and voluntary organizations, which are discussed below.

Major organizational changes were instituted within the ministry of health in 1982, when a new, comprehensive policy was adopted that began with the rudiments of health care by giving priority to (1) rural over urban health care; (2) preventive over curative care; (3) ambulatory care over hospitalization; and (4) public general hospitals over private or tertiary-care hospitals. Primary health care was given center stage in the newly revised health policy. But, perhaps the most innovative aspect of the new health strategy was the incorporation of medical education into the ministry of health, which was renamed the ministry of health and medical education (MOHME) in 1985. With this policy in place, medical education became more responsive to national health policy (see Underwood 1993 for a detailed discussion of this change).

A decision to devote nearly 50 percent of the health budget and a significant portion of health personnel to preventive care must be backed by resolute political will. The revolution brought with it that political will as is evidenced by changes in national health policy that followed in the revolution's wake. The commitment to primary care was reinforced in 1985 when the Majlis[4] set aside U.S. $40 million specifically for PHC, then doubled it the following year. This funding continues and is above and beyond the national health budget.

Primary health care receives support, in part, because its basic principles are in concordance with doctrinaire Islamic concerns regarding equity and universal participation. The revolutionary call to support the *mostaz'afin*—the disadvantaged or oppressed[5] segment of the population—was used to gain support for PHC as well as for other social programs. This initiative is part of an overall governmental policy that emphasizes rural advancement both as a vital part of its development strategy and as an Islamic moral obligation. The PHC network is important because it represents a long-term commitment to the provision of basic health services to those segments of the population who have the least access to private physicians—whether due to geographical location or inability to pay. But, it does not function in isolation. Two of the institutions that have been most effective in helping to realize the objectives of the primary health network are the mosque and Jihad-e Sazandegi, or the Reconstruction Crusade (RC).

The Mosque Network

In the months prior to the downfall of the Shah, the institution of the mosque was politicized and mobilized to an extent previously unknown. With the advent of the new government, the mosque could not be expected to revert to its former, less-active role. The mosque network is an organic part of Iranian life and reaches into the smallest villages and most remote outposts. It is an indigenous system well suited to information and policy dissemination. The mutual distrust that obtained between the clergy and the old regime precluded the use of that network for the advancement of government policies in the prerevolutionary era. Following the revolution, the mosque network has been used to promote governmental policies in the area of health as well as in politics.

Friday prayers have been among the most important forums for the dissemination of the dominant ideology. The Friday prayer has two segments: In the first, ethical issues are examined, and the content is largely determined by individual clergy. The second segment, the central theme of which is set by Tehran, is used to promote specific policies, whether of domestic or international concern.[6] The government-controlled media promotes the weekly message, intended not only for those who participate in Friday prayers. Friday prayers, invoking Qur'anic verses and hadith, have been used to advocate breast-feeding, immunization, basic hygienic practices, and literacy. Local mosques are also used for the allocation of food coupons, for the distribution of goods for the needy, and as centers to organize volunteers for a variety of projects.

The Reconstruction Crusade

Many institutions were established to provide social and public welfare. Primary among these is the Jihad-e Sazandegi,[7] or Reconstruction Crusade (RC), founded in 1979. Staffed initially by enthusiastic volunteers who were inspired by the call to serve Islam, the Reconstruction Crusade soon gained ministerial status. It was established to improve the lives of the 45 percent of the population who, at the time of the revolution, lived in about sixty thousand villages.[8]

The guiding principle of the RC is the Qur'anic verse that calls for Muslims to work in pairs or individually to effect good works. Youthful volunteers, as well as young men who have chosen to work for the RC to fulfill part of their military obligation, continue to constitute an important part of the organization. While its primary function has been to improve Iran's agriculture, the organization began almost immediately after the revolution to give other important services to rural Iranians, including electricity, roads, clean water, and sanitation systems, thereby making important contributions to the health status of many rural Iranians. Moreover, the RC built more than two thousand health clinics and several thousand public baths before the establishment of the PHC network in 1984 (Statistical Center of Iran 1986).

The Primary Health Care Network

In 1978, the International Conference on Primary Health Care (PHC), jointly sponsored by the World Health Organization (WHO) and UNICEF, convened at Alma-Ata in the Soviet Union. The document drawn up as a result of that conference, known as the Declaration of Alma-Ata, stated, in sum, that primary care is essential health care that includes education, promotion of basic food production and nutrition, potable water and sewage disposal, maternal and child care, immunizations, prevention and control of locally endemic disease, simplified care of common diseases and injuries, and provision of essential drugs.

In 1984, the Iranian PHC network, based on the WHO–UNICEF model, was formally established, thereby consolidating health services that had been overseen or provided by a diverse array of public and private organizations. For the rural population, the heart of the system is the *khaneh behdasht*, or health house, which serves as many as fifteen hundred people from the village in which they are located as well as the populations of designated satellite villages. Prior to the revolution, there were fewer than 800 health houses; by 1990, there were approximately 7,500 health houses, and, ten years later, the network had 15,000 health houses. Nearly 85 percent of villagers and 100 percent of urban dwellers have access to the network (Dungas 2000).[9]

One or two health care workers (HCW) staff each health house. When two health care workers are present, duties are generally gender specific, although not rigidly enforced. The female HCW is responsible for basic maternal and child health, including breast-feeding, weaning advice, and family planning, as well as treatment of minor illnesses, the administration of oral rehydration therapy, growth monitoring, and immunizations. The male HCW is in charge of environmental sanitation, potable water, and the control of communicable diseases. Thus, the PHC network encompasses both individual and public health benefits and functions as the coordinating mechanism for these services, particularly in rural areas.

Individuals who need a physician's attention are referred to a rural health center, which serves five to seven thousand people (or approximately five health houses). Urban residents have access to PHC through urban health centers. In 2000, there were approximately 4,500 rural and urban health centers in Iran. These centers provide integrated preventive and curative care, as well as referrals. Some provinces have now included mental health services as part of the PHC system. In addition to a physician, the rural health center is staffed with a health care associate, a health educator, a lab technician, a nurse, a midwife, and, often, a dental hygienist. In 1990, 95 percent of physicians in rural areas were foreigners, primarily from the Indian subcontinent. In interviews, many of these physicians reported that they have seen major improvements in the level of health-related knowledge among the villagers. Several of the rural physicians we interviewed in 1990 had been in Iran nearly ten years; they reported considerable improvements in health knowledge as well as in health practices among villagers over that time period. By 2002, all physicians in the PHC system were Iranians or were married to Iranian nationals.

Rural health centers are equipped with a few hospital beds for emergencies and severe cases of diarrhea, basic x-ray equipment, a lab, dental equipment, and a pharmacy. The pharmacies carry only generic drugs but seem to be well stocked. Health houses together with rural health centers constitute the primary level of care in rural areas, where all services are free of charge. Participation in the referral system is encouraged by the provision of free maternity care for women who are referred through their health house.

Public Health Outcomes

A compelling argument can be made that Islamic values and traditional institutions have influenced the formation and implementation of Iran's current health policy. But can the argument be taken one step further: namely, did health policy have a positive and demonstrable effect on health outcomes?

INFANT AND CHILD MORTALITY

As figure 1 indicates, infant mortality was reduced by 21 percent during the 1960s, by 34 percent in the 1970s, by 39 percent in the 1980s, and by another 44 percent in the 1990s. In short, the postrevolutionary period has seen a much more rapid decline in infant mortality than was true of the two prerevolutionary decades. Similarly, the under-five mortality rate dropped more precipitously in the postrevolutionary period than during the two decades prior to the revolution; moreover, the decline was faster than would have been predicted by pre-revolutionary trends.

During the 1980s, the Iranian infant mortality rate (IMR) was reduced in the face of economic decline and one of the highest rates of population growth in the world (UNICEF 1990). Between 1978 and 1990, the population increased nearly 40 percent. A population increase of this magnitude in such a short period

---

Figure 1: Infant & Under-five Mortality Rates*
in Iran, 1960–2000

	1960	1970	1980	1990	2000
infants	169	134	89	54	30
under five	281	199	130	72	38

*Deaths per 1,000 live births
Sources: 1960–1990: UNICEF; 2000 Demographic & Health Survey of the Islamic Republic of Iran (DHS/IRI)

places major stains on the health care infrastructure as well as on other public services. Moreover, it has negative implications for the well-being of individual mothers and infants, as it indicates short intervals between births as well as large families. Given an average inflation rate of over 20 percent[10] experienced in Iran during the late 1980s together with the press of a young, rapidly growing population, an increase in IMR might have been expected. That IMR did not increase, but continued to decline, is a tribute to the "safety net" effect of the PHC network.[11]

While the PHC system was formally inaugurated only in 1984, important health interventions had begun soon after the consolidation of the revolution. But PHC represents more than increased access to health services. It also brings with it a commitment to provide potable water, sanitation, and control of locally endemic diseases. The positive effects of expanded health services were bolstered by other government programs, including, but not limited to, expansion and reconstruction of the agricultural infrastructure, increased food subsidies, an ongoing literacy campaign, and extensive road construction in rural districts.

The data suggest that health-enhancing strategies undertaken during the early years of the revolution resulted in significant improvements in the overall health status of Iranian infants and children. Alternatively, a somewhat different explanation might be advanced: namely, that the effects of a rapidly expanding economy during the mid-1970s, in tandem with health programs implemented in the last years of the Shah's regime, were felt only after the revolution. In other words, "revolution" and "improved health status" are concomitant, but not causally, related. Certainly, the development projects of the former regime registered some positive results, as shown in figure 1.

Yet, a closer examination of the data belies that explanation. Since IMR, by definition, concerns infants during the first year of life, few health policy interventions have lag effects of any duration. In other words, health policy interventions must be sustained if they are to continue to show positive outcomes. The only exception could be with respect to the health of mothers. If the overall health status of mothers improved as a result of prerevolutionary health initiatives, it would be manifest in data revealing that neonatal mortality (deaths during the first twenty-eight days of life) had decreased significantly faster than had IMR, since improvement in mothers' health has the greatest impact on newborns. The data, however, show that the ratio of neonatal deaths to IMR has remained basically consistent (Malik Afzali 1989). Moreover, those factors that have been shown most effective in the reduction of IMR—such as access to clean water, immunizations, oral rehydration therapy, and prenatal care—were, for the most part, extended to the rural population after 1979. For these reasons, it is logical to conclude that the public health measures initiated during the present government's tenure have had impressive results and that the existence of a well-established national PHC network has provided—and continues to provide—systematic, ongoing access to basic and preventive health services.

WATER AND SANITATION

The 2000 Demographic and Health Survey/Islamic Republic of Iran (DHS/IRI) reports that 97 percent of the urban population and 86 percent of the rural population live in households with clean drinking water, which represents a 20-point increase over 1990 for rural residents. (Urban access to clean drinking water was already at 95 percent in 1990.) Approximately 86 percent of urban, but only 47 percent of rural residents have hygienic or semihygienic toilets. These percentages can be contrasted with the year before the revolution, when more than 90 percent of Iranian villagers had neither clean water nor acceptable sanitation systems. The provision of potable water and sanitation systems is the joint responsibility of the MOHME and the ministry of the Reconstruction Crusade.

IMMUNIZATION

Immunization coverage has improved markedly. Before 1980, coverage of the six major vaccines for children under one year of age ranged from 5 to 25 percent. By 1984, the year during which the Expanded Program on Immunization (EPI) was introduced, approximately 60 percent of children under one year of age had received diphtheria, tetanus, pertussis (DPT); Bacillus Calmette-Guérin (BCG), preventive therapy for mycobacterium and tuberculosis; polio; and measles vaccines. At that time, urban coverage was generally more thorough than in rural areas. Official sources continued to report very high coverage during the war years, indicating that by 1990 coverage was near 95 percent. In international development circles, there was considerable doubt that the immunization rates could have been maintained at such a high level. Yet, subsequent data confirmed that these percentages were accurate; by 1999, UNICEF estimated that coverage had reached 99 percent (UNICEF 1999). The 2000 DHS/IRI confirmed those findings (Iranian Statistics Centre 2002). While occasional immunization campaigns can bring about high coverage rates temporarily, the PHC system provides an ongoing health-delivery system to maintain a relatively high level of coverage. Seventy percent of the vaccines are produced in Iran.

Policy Changes during the Second Postrevolutionary Decade

The notable successes in reducing infant and child mortality and improving immunization rates, access to clean water, and proper sanitation, which were clearly evident at the end of the first postrevolutionary decade, quickened during the second decade. Yet, there were weaknesses in the system that clearly needed redress.

At 3.8 percent, Iran's population growth rate was inordinately high during the 1980s, community participation in health improvement was limited—preventive as well as curative services

were considered largely the responsibility of paid paraprofessionals and professionals—and the nutritional status of mothers and
children demanded attention.

FAMILY PLANNING

Iran experienced a rapid, possibly unequaled, decline in the total
fertility rate (TFR) between 1984, when TFR stood at 6.4, and
2000, by which time it had fallen to 2.0 (2000 DHS/IRI). There
has been much discussion in the literature about the causes of
this precipitous decline. While much credit has been given to
the government's antinatalist policy, which was set forth in a bill
passed by the Majlis in 1991, it is important to note that the TFR
actually began to decline in the mid-1980s, having dropped to 5.5
by 1988 (Abbasi-Shavazi 2001). The antinatalist policy was—and
continues to be—an important factor. Yet the widespread health
improvements brought about through the PHC network in tandem
with broad socioeconomic improvements in rural areas, which
have been discussed above, certainly created an atmosphere con-
ducive to smaller family size.

The antinatalist policy was important because it not only
led to improved access to contraceptive methods but gave rise
to communication campaigns that promoted small families. A
latent demand for contraception was clearly in place before the
antinatalist policy was legislated. While the promotional media
campaigns helped establish family planning as a social norm and
the well-established health network greatly facilitated delivery of
methods, the acclivitous rise in the contraceptive prevalence rate
(CPR) from 49 percent in 1989 to 74 percent in 2000 resulted
also from delayed marriage and the desire for fewer children. In-
terestingly, modern method use among urban and rural women is
similar at 55 percent and 57 percent, respectively. Approximately
22 percent of urban and 10 percent of rural women use traditional
methods. Although Muslim religious leaders in Jordan and Egypt,
among other predominantly Muslim countries, oppose the use

of tubal ligation and vasectomy on religious grounds, the Iranian
'ulama have stated that permanent methods are acceptable (Underwood 2000). As shown in figure 2, approximately 15 percent
of married women report that they rely on male methods; over
one-third of married women who rely on modern methods report
that they or their spouses have undergone sterilization.

COMMUNITY HEALTH VOLUNTEERS

MOHME senior officials and their staffs were forthcoming in con-
versations with me in the summer of 1990 regarding the gap in
coverage of some low-income urban residents. Health workers
in rural areas know all members of their catchment areas and
are proactive in reaching those who do not seek preventive care;
this was often not true in more densely populated urban areas.
To remedy this situation, the ministry developed a program for
community health volunteers (CHVs) who would serve as interme-
diaries between urban health centers and periurban communities.
The program went to scale in 1993, staffed by women who were
literate, of reproductive age, and trusted by their communities.

Figure 2. Contraceptive Method Use Reported by Married Iranian Women Who Rely on Modern Methods, 2000

Male Sterilization	5%
Norplant	1%
Injections	5%
Condoms	10%
IUDs	15%
Female Sterlization	31%
Pills	33%

Source: Iranian Ministry of Health and Education et al., Demographic
and Health Surveys, Islamic Republic of Iran 2000. (Tehran: MOHME,
2002).

These criteria were important as the CHVs must have easy access to women of reproductive age, be trusted by their neighbors to keep private matters private, and be able to read, understand, and communicate health information to the fifty households assigned to her. By 2002, the force had grown to some fifty thousand volunteers.

A detailed curriculum has been developed for the CHVs, who meet weekly at their local urban health center to learn about specific health topics, to discuss pressing health issues, and to share their experiences. During interviews with two groups of CHVs in Tabriz in the summer of 2002, I heard many stories about the empowering effects of participation in the program. One woman recounted her success in convincing the municipality to repave a road in her neighborhood, which she argued was a hazard. Anecdotal evidence of the program's success was reinforced by an evaluation study carried out by the MOHME in 1994–1995, which found that members of communities with CHVs were more knowledgeable about health matters and were more likely to take positive action than were people in neighborhoods that did not have CHVs (MOHME and UNICEF 1998).

Conclusions

The strides Iran has made as a result of the expansive PHC network are impressive. Many nations lack any semblance of a PHC system and their health-status indicators remain poor. The Iranian approach, which has focused primarily on access to care and, secondarily, on those elements of PHC that can be set in motion relatively quickly, provides valuable lessons for other nations that hope to implement a similar system. Ideally, PHC should be implemented as a total program with all elements present from the beginning. Realistically, this is very difficult to achieve. The strengths as well as the weaknesses of this strategy can be instructive for other nation-states.

Improved health status has been explained as primarily

(1) a byproduct of social and economic development or (2) an outcome of social-policy interventions and technological innovations. A comparison of pre- and postrevolutionary Iran may shed light on the relative efficacy of these two approaches.[12] Under the monarchy, Iranian development strategies did not include broad-based, nationwide health initiatives directed specifically at the poor and disadvantaged populations. Yet, infant mortality rates were reduced (see figure 1). In that period, Iran experienced rapid economic growth. Per capita income increased nearly threefold in the ten-year period from 1968 to 1978. Health-status improvement, then, was primarily a byproduct of economic development. In the postrevolutionary period, social and health policies designed explicitly to improve the lot of the mostaz'afin were instituted. Additionally, technological innovations, such as immunization and oral rehydration therapy, have been used more systematically than was true prior to the revolution. Health status, as measured by infant and child mortality rates, improved even more dramatically than under the former government. This case, therefore, supports the contention that social policy and the quest for equity, as part of a larger development strategy, can produce positive results more quickly than does an economic development strategy that focuses first on growth, then on distribution of social and economic resources.

The PHC system, which relies on female as well as male health care workers, is an important means to empower people at the grassroots. The introduction of community health volunteers (CHVs) in urban areas served to complement the PHC network even as it offered another route to empowerment. It demonstrates that local people can be responsible for their own health and that women are vital to that process, not merely as passive recipients of health care but as proactive participants. In a religiously imbued country, such as Iran, the provision of public health services in the name of Islam lends a certain legitimacy to the system as a whole, including the role that women play. Equally important, the implementation of a nationwide PHC network must be viewed within the larger context of overall economic development. Health is a relatively nonthreatening sphere in which community participation can evolve as a natural part of life. Once established, the tradition of self-reliance and self-determination can have important positive consequences for the success of other development projects. This was demonstrated in two group interviews with nearly forty CHVs that I conducted in the summer of 2002, discussed above.

Public health services in rural areas of Iran have improved during the tenure of the current regime. Despite successful PHC pilot projects in the provinces of Fars and West Azerbaijan in the 1970s, a commitment to rural public health services was missing. The revolution brought with it the social vision and political will, previously absent, that could provide a foundation for primary health care. This resolve was expressed in terms of Islam but is not unique to Islam; similar improvements in access to health care have been observed in other countries that have experienced a fundamental shift in the power structure. Nevertheless, the Iranian case demonstrates that Islamic principles and beliefs can be used to further development activities. The equitable distribution of health services is grounded in the tenets of Islam. While an organization such as Jihad-e Sazandegi, born of the revolution, might be expected to use ideology to intensify its appeal, it is clear that even the health bureaucracy has been influenced by, or found it useful to espouse, Islamic concepts.

Policymakers who hope to effect change in Muslim countries must be fully cognizant of the potential uses of Islamic discourse in policy implementation. On one hand, sermons, coordinated by Tehran and delivered at Friday prayer services throughout the country, were used to encourage breast-feeding, immunizations, and hygienic practices. On the other hand, the same mosque network was used through most of the 1980s to discourage contraceptive use. Yet, once convinced that specific policies are compatible with Islamic principles, Muslim religious leaders are particularly effective in policy dissemination—as so clearly attested by the dramatic change in Iran's family-planning policy and the rapid reduction in the population growth rate.

Whether the clergy are successful in a given situation will be tempered by their ability to describe such policies in a manner that is in keeping with their audiences' belief systems and perceived needs. Before policymakers select the Muslim clergy as an appropriate instrument for policy implementation, however, a thorough assessment must be made of how the clergy are received in any given situation. In some regions, other community leaders may be equally or even more effective in development projects.

Muslim people, regardless of their sectarian persuasion, share basic doctrines, convictions, and mores that exert direct and indirect influence on private and public life. Though organizational details of the mosque networks in other Muslim countries differ from the system in Iran, the mosque remains an integral part of Muslim daily life. The 'ulama often have the authority to win acceptance among the most traditional segments of the population for programs and policies that initially may face opposition. Moreover, in this era of Muslim resurgence, policies that are shown to be concordant with Islam can secure legitimacy across a broad sector of the population.

In the decades since the Iranian revolution, the world has witnessed a marked increase in sociopolitical movements that claim to act within Islamic principles. Islamic discourse, therefore, must be analyzed and understood if policymakers hope to effect change among peoples who profess Islam. It is hoped that documentation of the revolutionary Iranian regime's impact on public health will contribute to a more lucid understanding of this process. The Iranian case is particularly important, for this strategically located country, whose rhetoric and policies have been informed by Islamic ideology, continues to have influence and consequences beyond its territorial borders.

Notes

1. This chapter is based on fieldwork conducted in Iran during the summers of 1990, 1991, and 2002 together with statistical findings from nationally representative surveys conducted in Iran over the period of interest.

2. See Assar and Jaksic 1975; King 1983; and Andreano 1984 for a full discussion of these pilot projects.

3. For the Shi'a, the traditions are based on the actions and sayings of the Twelve Imams, all of whom were descendants of the Prophet, as well as on those of the Prophet.

4. The Majlis is the Iranian unicameral parliament and is elected by the direct vote of the people.

5. The term "oppressed" is used in Iran primarily to refer to those who are economically disadvantaged, although the rural population is generally considered disadvantaged with respect to social and economic services.

6. The international press often reports these pronouncements.

7. The term *jihad* is derived from the Arabic root that means to struggle or to make an effort.

8. While the Reconstruction Crusade also provides services to urban areas, more than 80 percent of its resources are expended in rural areas.

9. Individuals who live within a six-kilometer radius of a health house are considered to have access.

10. UNICEF 1990.

11. As the IMR decreases, it becomes increasingly difficult to effect further significant reductions.

12. Though it can be argued that pre- and postrevolutionary Iran represent two different cases (Ragin 1987), the two cases are not independent, which raises Galton's problem (Hammel 1980, 147). To draw broad generalizations concerning the causes of improved health status, it would be necessary to introduce at least one other case for the purposes of comparison. That objective, however, would take us beyond the scope of this paper.

Bibliography

Abbasi-Shavazi, Mohammad Jalal. 2001. "The Fertility Revolution in Iran." *Population & Societies*, no. 373 (November).

Andreano, Ralph. 1984. "Some Personal Observations on Health Policy in Iran, 1973–1978." *Social Science and Medicine* 19(1): 1–7.

Arjomand, Said Amir. 1988. *The Turban for the Crown: The Islamic Revolution in Iran.* Oxford: Oxford University Press.

Assar, M., and Z. Jaksic. 1975. "A Health Services Development Project in Iran." In *Health by the People,* edited by Kenneth W. Newell. Geneva: World Health Organization.

Cornia, Giovanni Andrea, Richard Jolly, and Frances Stewart, eds. 1987. *Adjustment with a Human Face,* vol. 1 and 2. Oxford: Clarendon Press.

"Constitution of the Islamic Republic of Iran." *Middle East Journal* 34(2): 189.

Dungas, Abubakar. 2000. "Iran's Other Revolution." *Populi* 27(2).

Good, Byron J. 1981. "The Transformation of Health Care in Modern Iranian History." In *Continuity and Change in Modern Iran,* edited by Michael E. Bonine and Nikki R. Keddie. Albany: State University of New York Press, 1981.

Grant, John B. 1963. *Health Care for the Community: Selected Papers of Dr. John B. Grant.* Edited by Conrad Seipp. Baltimore: Johns Hopkins Press.

Gwatkin, Davidson R., Janet R. Wilcox, and Joe Wray. 1981. "Can Health and Nutrition Interventions Make a Difference?" *World Health Forum* 2(1): 119–28.

Hammel, E. A. 1980. "The Comparative Method in Anthropological Perspective." *Comparative Studies in Society and History* 22(2): 145–55.

Iranian Statistics Centre. 2002. *Demographic and Health Survey of the Islamic Republic of Iran, October 2000.* Tehran: Ministry of Health and Medical Education.

Khomeini, Imam (Ruhollah). 1981. *Islam and Revolution.* Translated and annotated by Hamid Algar. Berkeley: Mizan Press.

King, Maurice. 1983. *An Iranian Experiment in Primary Health Care: The West Azerbaijan Project.* Oxford: Oxford University Press.

Malik Afzali, Hossain. 1989. *Evaluation of Birth and Death Indicators in the Islamic Republic of Iran 1988.* Tehran: Iranian MOHME.

McKeown, T. 1976. *The Role of Medicine: Dream, Mirage, or Nemesis?* London: Nuffield Provincial Hospitals Trust.

Ministry of Health and Medical Education and UNICEF. 1998. *Community Health Volunteers in Iran: Women as Agents of Health and Development in the Islamic Republic of Iran.* Tehran: MOHME and UNICEF.

Preston, S. H. 1978. "Causes and Consequences of Mortality Declines in

Less Developed Countries during the Twentieth Century." In *Population and Economic Change in Developing Countries*, edited by Easterlin. Washington, D.C.: National Bureau of Economic Research.

Ragin, Charles C. 1987. *The Comparative Method*. Berkeley: University of California Press.

Rahman, Fazlur. 1987. *Health and Medicine in the Islamic Tradition*. New York: Cross Road.

Ronaghy, Hossain A., and S. Solten. 1972. "Is the Chinese 'Barefoot Doctor' Exportable to Rural Iran." *Lancet* 29(June): 1331–3.

Sidel, Victor, and Ruth Sidel. 1977. "Primary Health Care in Relation to Socio-Political Structure." *Social Science and Medicine* 11: 415–9.

Swenson, Ingrid. 1977. "Expected Reductions in Fetal and Infant Mortality by Prolonged Pregnancy Spacing in Rural Bangladesh." *Bangladesh Development Studies* 5(1): 1–16.

Statistical Center of Iran. 1986, 1987, 1988. *Statistical Yearbook, Iranian National Census*. Tehran, Iran.

Underwood, Carol. 1993. "A Quiet Revolution: Primary Health Care in Rural Iran." In *Global Learning for Health*, edited by Russell Morgan Jr. and William Rau, 85–96. Washington, D.C.: National Council for International Health.

———. 2000. "Islamic Precepts and Family Planning: Contrasting the Perceptions of Jordanian Religious Leaders and Their Constituents." *International Family Planning Perspectives* 26(3): 110–7, 136.

UNICEF. 1988. *Statistics on Children in UNICEF Assisted Countries*. New York: UNICEF Publications.

———. 1990. *Situation Analysis of Children and Women in Iran*. New York: UNICEF Publications.

United Nations. 1980. *Population and Vital Statistical Report, Statistical Papers*. New York.

World Bank. 1989. *World Development Report 1989*. Oxford University Press for the World Bank.

WHO (World Health Organization). 1986. *Repercussions of the World Economic Situation*. Provisional Report by the Director-general, 39th World Health Assembly, A39/4, 1986.

WHO/UNICEF. 1978. "Primary Health Care." In *Report of the International Conference on Primary Health Care*, 6. Alma-Ata, USSR, September 6–12, 1978.

———. 1999. *Review of National Immunization Coverage: 1980–1999*.

Glossary of Arabic Terms

'ada: Custom, tradition.

akham: Five Islamic rulings or orders, including *wajib* (obligatory), *halal* (recommended), *mubah* (acceptable), *makruh* (not forbidden, but undesirable), and *haram* (forbidden or religiously proscribed).

al-Azhar: World's oldest university; Sunni Islam's foremost seat of learning.

ayatollah: A high rank in the Shi'ite hierarchy of religious scholars; the most respected scholars are known as the grand ayatollahs. If one exceptional scholar's opinions dominate, he is known as *Marja-i Taqlid.* (These terms are not current among Sunni Muslims.)

'azl: Contraception by withdrawal before ejaculation; coitus interruptus.

bay'a: Pledge of allegiance to a leader.

faqih: (plural *fuqaha'*) Jurist, a person who is trained in the discipline of Islamic jurisprudence (fiqh).

fatwa: Formal legal decision or opinion proffered by a *mufti,* a *mujtahid,* or another of the *'ulama* with sufficient standing.

fiqh: Islamic jurisprudence, legal discourse, insight.

ghayla: The small assassination; damage done by the diversion of nutrients after a woman becomes pregnant while nursing a child.

hadd: A particular punishment for violating Islamic law.

hadith: Teachings, sayings, or actions of the Prophet Muhammad. A written account or tradition (Sunna) of the prophet that explains, applies, and elaborates the Qur'an.

hijab: From the root *hajaba*, which means to veil or hide from sight. Hajab refers to the Islamic dress code which obligates every Muslim woman to cover her body from head to foot, except for the face and hands. This dress code is variously interpreted and practiced in Muslim countries around the world. Most agree that hijab requires a woman to cover her hair, though a minority contends that modesty is internal and does not necessarily imply a head cover. In some countries, women who practice hijab wear a head scarf and loose clothing, such as slacks and a loose shirt or a jacket and a long skirt. During prayer and the *hajj* (pilgrimage), women are forbidden to cover their faces or their hands.

idda: Prescribed period of waiting during which a woman cannot remarry after being widowed or divorced. The purpose of idda is to determine paternity if the woman is pregnant. The length of this waiting period is four months and ten days for a widow and three menstrual periods for a divorced woman.

ijtihad: A jurist's *(mujtahid)* exhaustive effort to uncover or deduce the law in a novel or unprecedented case using Islamic sources (Qur'an, Sunna, ijma') by independent reasoning.

ijma': Consensus of scholars or Muslim jurists and judges; the third authoritative source for Islamic law after the Qur'an and Sunna.

imam: For the Sunnis, any male member of the community who leads a congregational prayer. For the Shi'ites, a descendant of Ali who led the Shi'ite community with infallible guidance from God. A religious leader who leads the community in political affairs is also called an imam.

Islamists: An English term or title used for Muslim political activists; individuals who actively utilize Islam in the political sphere.

istislah: Seeking the best solution for the general interest or public welfare.

khul': Divorce by mutual consent, initiated and demanded by the wife, who then abandons her claim to the marriage gift or the alimony.

madrassas: From the Arabic word, *madaris,* meaning "schools." In some non-Arabic speaking countries, religious schools are called *madrassas* or *deeni madari.*

mahr: Money, jewelry, or a symbolic gift given to the bride by the groom; bride-price.

makruh: The fourth *ahkam* (ruling) literally means detested, reprehensible, or blameworthy, i.e., an action better to be avoided than to be committed.

mufti : An Islamic scholar who gives legal opinion concerning Islamic law.

mujtahid: A person who exercises ijithad; authoritative interpreter of the law.

Qur'an: Believed by Muslims to be God's (Allah's) last revelation to mankind, revealed in the Arabic language to Prophet Muhammad; the scripture of Islam; the most authoritative document in Islam and source of Islamic teachings and laws.

sahib-e-nisab: A Muslim who has money beyond the limit prescribed under Islamic law, and who is therefore obligated to pay a certain percentage to the needy.

shari'a: Islamic law; the correct path of action as determined by God.

Sheikh al-Azhar: Title given to the rector of al-Azhar University in Cairo, who was generally regarded as an important scholar of the religious sciences.

Shi'a or Shi'ites: Muslims who believe that the only legitimate leadership rests in the lineage of Muhammad's cousin and son-in-law,' Ali. Shi'ites represent a minority of Muslims worldwide, but a majority in Iran, Iraq, and Lebanon.

Sufi: One who believes in Sufism, a mystic school of thought that is separate from mainstream Islam.

Sunna: The teachings, sayings, manners, and actions of the Prophet Muhammad transmitted through the written reports of the hadith.

Sunni: A follower of the Qur'an and the Sunna, representing the majority of Muslims worldwide. It is implied that a Muslim is Sunni unless he or she specifies otherwise.

talaq al-bidah: An irregular form of divorce, when the husband repudiates his wife by saying three times in succession:"I divorce you." The Muslim who divorces his wife in this way is considered to be an offender of Islamic law, but the divorce still takes legal effect.

talaq al-sunna: The preferred method of divorce, when the husband pronounces once to his nonpregnant wife,"I divorce you" in front of two witnesses.

'ulama: Religious scholars, literally the people of knowledge; the top of a hierarchy of men trained in Islamic religious science and Arabic language. (Singular *'alim*).

'urf: Custom.

ushr: The act of charging and collecting interest on loans, which is prohibited by Islam.

wa'd: Pre-Islamic practice of exposing unwanted female children to the elements; female infanticide.

waqf: The permanent dedication, by a person professing Islam, of property of any kind for any purpose recognized as religious, pious, or charitable. (Plural *awqaf*).

zakat (or zakah): One of the five pillars of Islam, the obligatory transfer of wealth, also called "alms due." All Muslims who own more wealth than the limit prescribed under Islamic law are obligated to give a certain percentage, the zakah, to charitable activities to improve the living standards of poor Muslims.

Contributors

Stephen P. Heyneman received his Ph.D. in Comparative Education from the University of Chicago in 1975. Currently, he is Professor of International Education Policy at Peabody College, Vanderbilt University. For twenty-one years, prior to joining the Vanderbilt faculty, he helped design and manage education programs at the World Bank.

Ahmad Dallal is Associate Professor of Islamic Studies at Georgetown University in Washington D.C. He taught at Smith College, Yale University, and Stanford University. He received his PhD in Islamic Studies from Columbia University in 1990 and has authored numerous articles on the history of Islamic science, Islamic law, and Islamic revivalist thought. He is currently finishing a book-length comparative study of eighteenth-century Islamic reform entitled *Islam Without Europe: Traditions of Reform in Eighteenth-Century Islamic Thought.*

Donna Lee Bowen received her Ph.D. from the University of Chicago in Near Eastern Languages and Civilizations in 1981. Currently, she is Professor of Political Science and Middle Eastern Studies at Brigham Young University and publishes on questions of politics, religion, and social policy in North Africa and the Middle East.

Gail Richardson received her Master's degree in Public Administration from New York University in 1990. She is currently consulting for the World Health Organization in Manila, The Philippines. Previously she was a senior health specialist at the World Bank, working primarily on children's health programs in the Middle East and North Africa.

Carol Underwood is a sociologist specializing in international health and communication for social development. She received her Ph.D. from Johns Hopkins University in 1993 and is currently Senior Associate in the Department of Population and Family Health Sciences and the Center for Communication Programs at the Johns Hopkins School of Public Health.

Index

abortion:
    legal status of, 138, 142, 146
    Muslim views on, 130–32
Abu-Lughod, 103, 106–7
Afghanistan, 126
Al-Azhar University, 119
Algeria, 36, 76, 94, 138
Ayatollah Khomeini, 132–33, 138
banks:
    Allied Bank of Pakistan Ltd., 161
    Habib Bank Limited, 161
    Muslim Commercial Bank, 161
    National Bank of Pakistan, 161
    The State Bank of Pakistan, 161
    United Bank Limited, 161
    World Bank, 2
birth control:
    arguments against, 136–37, 140, 142
    consequences of, 140
    methods of, 5, 129
    role of, 122
brotherhood, 93, 139, 185
contraception:
    'azl, 127
    legal position on, 148
    opinions about, 128
    prohibition of, 133
    and role of women, 137
    study of, 146

    support for, 146
    and well-being of the family, 122
contract:
    civil, 59
    importance of, 6
    law, 56, 88, 122
    marriage. *See* marriage.
    waqf, 22, 31
divorce:
    and Hanafi law, 63
    husband's power to, 76
    laws governing, 62
    one-sided, 62
    the right to seek, 49, 52, 58–59, 64, 74–75, 77, 94, 96
    role of custom in, 106
    and Shi'i law, 63
education:
    formal, 159–60
    grant-in-aid for, 177,
    higher, 145
    Islamic, 9, 101
    medical, 184, 189
    rehabilitation through, 163
    religious, 3, 9, 142, 171
    special, 164, 165, 176
    system of, 101
    value of, 55,
    western, 9, 101
    of women, 93, 96

educational:
  curricula, 133
  institutions, 85, 159, 162, 169–71,
    176
  policies, 55
  practice, 8
  status of men, 55
  vocational, 158
Egypt, 78–79, 85, 94, 106–8, 126,
  134–35, 139, 170
family:
  economic obligations, 61
  Iranian Protection Law, 77
  Iran's Family Protection Act, 94
  law, 50, 56–59, 70, 83, 92, 94, 96,
    100, 147
  Muhammad's, 123, 127
  order, 89, 92
  planning, 55, 92, 94, 118, 120–23,
    127, 133–34, 137–38, 140–49,
    192, 198, 203
  property, 66, 104
  reform in, 70, 92, 94, 96, 98
  rights, 103
  roles, 47, 88
  size, 142, 144, 149, 198
  structure, 58, 111, 121
  waqf, 15, 18, 23, 36–37
foundations:
  Byzantine/Christian, 14
  charitable, 28
  Fauju, 163
  National Zakat Foundation, (NZF)
    164, 166
  Pakistan Model Education
    Institutions, 174, 177
  Waqf, 16
Hamas, 139
health policy, 182, 189, 194–95
India, 37, 70, 77, 126, 193
inheritance:
  female, 50
  intergenerational, 3
  law of, 3, 27, 29, 36, 47, 64–65, 78,
    103
  need of, 57

principles of, 4
reforms of, 78
regulation of, 53
rights for, 50, 65, 78, 88
studies on, 65
Sunni law on, 78
institutions:
  for the care of the handicapped, 169
  charitable, 166
  educational, 162, 169–71, 175–76
  financial, 161
  of health, 159, 174–75, 177
  Islamic. See Islamic.
  Jihad-e Sazandegi (Reconstruction
    Crusade (RC), 190–91
  model, 176
  Mosque, 190
  public, 178
  publicly financed, 178
  religious, 168, 176
  restoration, of 170
  serving the poor, 164
  training, 164
  of waqf, 168–69
  welfare, 161, 164
Iran, Islamic Republic, 35, 64, 71, 73,
  76–77, 94, 106, 112, 119–20,
  133, 138, 142, 182–85, 187, 190,
  197–203
Islam:
  apostasy for, 68
  authority of, 122
  choice of, 72
  contemporary, 44, 114, 149
  core practices of, 83
  ethical principles of, 71
  five pillars of, 69
  focus of, 120
  and health policy, 181
  law of, 122
  position on women, 82, 89, 94, 100,
    103, 108, 112
  principals of, 126
  reforms of, 49
  renunciation of, 63
  scholars of, 119, 120

schools of, 125, 160
Shi'ite, 143,
social values of, 156,
sources of, 84, 91, 95, 123, 185
Sunni, 125
Islamic:
    activists, 74, 139
    Algerian Salvation Front, 138
    association, 139
    awqaf (waqf), 2, 15, 170
    concept, 9, 168, 174, 202
    countries (nations), 35–36, 109, 157
    courts, 3
    culture, 1, 4, 99, 168
    dress, 94, 110
    history, 2, 66
    ideology, 185–88, 203
    institution, 180
    law, 3, 4, 5, 6, 13, 32, 34–36, 46–47,
        49, 56–57, 61, 64–75, 78–82,
        84, 88, 91, 95, 102, 104, 106,
        107, 110, 113, 119–20, 122–25,
        133, 139, 141, 146, 148, 149,
        156–57, 169
    legal norms, 37
    legal system, 14, 99, 111, 120
    legal tradition, 4
    legal mechanisms, 7
    malaysian party, 138
    political parties, 138
    practice, 105, 107,-108, 122, 127
    reform, 94, 96, 111
    Republic of Iran, 8, 181, 188
    scholars, 119–20
    schools of law, 23
    Shari'a, 68
    social policy, 4, 7
    values, 107, 119, 139, 149, 194
    views on women, 92, 112
    University, 119, 133
    world, 5, 44, 100, 168, 170
Islamist:
    activists, 82, 84, 91, 112
    Jordanian blocs, 138
    movements, 94

sentiments, 71
views on women's role, 92
women. See women.
Khomeini's Islamic Republic, 94
Lebanon, 138
Libya, 37, 94, 101, 134
marriage:
    and bride-price, 61
    contract, 52, 94, 130
    legal age for, 71–74
    plural, 73
    principles of, 5
    and property rights, 104–5
    repudiation of. See repudiation.
    requirements for women, 72
    the right to accept or reject, 59
    the right to construct, 57, 60, 73
    the right to dissolve. See divorce.
    and social status, 60
    temporary marriage, 61, 127
    values of, 6, 146
Mashhad al-Khalil, 15
Mauritania, 94
Morocco, 4, 27, 64, 72, 105, 134, 141,
    143, 170
Muhammad, prophet, 5, 15–17, 21, 48,
    50, 91, 110, 120–23, 126, 186
Musa Sadr, 138
Muslim activists, 44, 45, 82, 84, 91, 94,
    112, 140
Muslim Youth Movement of Malaysia,
    138
National Evacuee Trust Property Board
    (NETPB), 174–80
Pakistan, 72–73, 76–79, 94, 98, 101,
    119, 126, 138, 157, 161–64, 167–
    70, 174–80
polygamy:
    intellectual foundations for, 6, 96
    and Islamists position, 93–94
    and marriage reform, 72–73
    and modernists position, 96
    prohibition of, 54,
    restriction on, 92
    rights for, 50, 71

Pre-islamic:
   Arabia, 14, 50, 57, 58
   Arabs, 111
   cultural tradition, 4
   customs, 53, 68
   Matrelinian system, 107
   practice, 127
   times, 50, 5, 75
repudiation:
   of marriage, 52, 58, 68
   Islamic system of, 75
   rights for. See divorce.
Saudi Arabia, 55, 71, 79, 101, 119, 126,
   134, 139, 157
Shi'i:
   school of, 59, 126
   Muslims, 61
   Movement of the Deprived, 138
   law, 63, 66, 127
   inheritance, 77
sterilization:
   legal texts on, 132
   prohibition of, 132, 138, 146
   reports on, 199
Sub-Saharan Africa, 107
Sudan, 76–78, 94, 104, 106, 108, 157
Syria, 27, 37, 76–77, 139, 170
Takfir wal-Hegira, 139
Tunisia, 27, 37, 73, 76, 77–78, 94, 100,
   134, 138
westernization, 35, 45
women:
   activists, 92
   age of marriage for, 73
   behavior, 44
   circumcision of, 108
   conformity to ideal norms, 45
   and criminal law, 78–81
   and divorce, 63, 74, 76–77, 96

   dress of, 47, 92, 94, 97, 110
   education of. See education.
   Egyptian Muslim Association, 93
   equality of men and, 52, 75
   and family planning, 133–34
   inheritance, 64–67, 78
   Islamist, 94
   liberation of, 45, 92,
   maternity care for, 193
   Muslim, 7, 46–47, 56, 60, 82,
      92–93, 99, 108, 112
   Muslim's arguments on status of,
      82–84
   participation in pubic life, 89
   place in society, 44, 88
   position of, 4
   power of, 108–9
   rights for, 45, 53, 56, 67, 71, 75, 87,
      90, 96–99, 110
   status of, 44–45, 47–48, 50, 52,
      55–56, 73, 98, 100, 110
   submissiveness, 46
   subordination of, 52, 108
   treatment of, 3, 4, 53
   veiling of, 46, 110
   views on, 45, 86, 98–99
Yemen Arab Republic, 77
zakat:
   Central Fund, 157, 159, 162
   Central Council, 7, 158–60, 163,
      165
   definition of, 156
   Ministry of, 7
   National Zakat Foundation. See
      foundations.
   Provincial Council, 162
   Provincial Funds, 159, 161, 163
   reform in, 163